EARNING MONEY AT HOME

a Consumer Publication

edited by Edith Rudinger

published by Consumers' Association
publishers of **Which?**

Consumer Publications are
available from Consumers'
Association and from
booksellers. Titles of
other Consumer Publications
are given at the end of
this book.

© Consumers' Association July 1979

ISBN 0 85202 166 6

 Computer typeset
and printed offset litho
by Page Bros (Norwich) Ltd

a Consumer Publication

EARNING
MONEY
AT HOME

Consumers' Association
publishers of **Which?**
14 Buckingham Street
London WC2N 6DS

CONTENTS

WORKING AT HOME

There are practical advantages to working at home. You do not have to travel to work (although you may have to travel to get or dispose of your goods) so you have more time available, do not have to pay fares, go out in all weathers or worry about getting back by a certain time to collect children. When working at home, you do not need to wear 'good' clothes (although you may need to have one respectable outfit for when you go to see people about work) or have your hair done or shave. You can be in when the plumber calls, and be there to take in parcels from the postman. Should burglars be round your way (and many burglaries are carried out in the daytime), they are not likely to choose your house.

You are your own boss and can fit in your work at times to suit you and your clients—when the children or other members of the household are out during the day, or during the evening.

No one is going to stand over you and tell you what to do in detail. For some people, this is the main attraction of working on their own. But if you have been used to receiving instructions, you may find it is difficult at first to organise your own work, decide how long you can afford to spend on each item and make sure that you get it done. You may of necessity have to work late in the evenings even if you are tired or would like to watch television.

One of the disadvantages of working at home is that the work is always there, staring at you and reproaching you for not getting on with it while you are doing other things.

You have to be better organised to work at home than if you are going out to work. The work itself may take up space in the house and make the place untidy. The most important thing is to keep everything to do with your work entirely separate from other things around you at home. If you are at work in a place away from home, you can leave everything on your desk or bench at the end of the day, knowing that it will be there waiting for you the next morning. This is unlikely to be easy when you are working at home, especially if there are children about. Unless you have a separate room, you have to make sure that all work, tools and materials can be put away and kept somewhere when you are not using them. It is particularly important not to get work money mixed up with domestic money.

It requires a great deal of self-discipline to work at home: in many ways, it is much easier to go out to work, leaving household jobs undone and unseen behind you, than it is to stay and have to work with distractions around. When you are at home and your attention wanders from your work, it is only too easy to justify doing some domestic task like going to hang out the washing or mow the lawn, just because the sun is shining.

motives

Why you want to start working at home is a question you should ask yourself before embarking on any job, if only to make sure that you do want to work and that you do not set out to do something that you cannot do effectively.

Will your earnings be an essential part of the family budget? Do you need the money solely to keep up with the effects of inflation, or as pocket money, a useful but not essential addition to the family income? These factors will affect what you do, when you do it, how you prepare for doing it (including any refresher course you may take), how many hours you spend on it, and how desperate you feel about taking whatever work you can.

For a retired person or an under-occupied housewife perhaps earning money may not be the primary consideration. But a second breadwinner's earnings can start off as pin money and end up as something the family relies on to pay the gas/garage/holiday bill. If the money you earn is likely to become essential, you should not undertake work that is only seasonal or spasmodic unless this is the only way you can get started.

Your financial needs and motives play a paramount part in what you can afford to do and how long you can wait before breaking even or making a profit (however small). For some types of work, you would need some capital to begin with—for buying equipment, adapting your premises, getting in supplies or stock. And with some occupations, there is no likelihood of getting a cash return for quite some time after your investment.

what can you do?

Maybe there is an opportunity to convert an interest into a job or profession, or a hobby into a money-earning activity that gives you more satisfaction than conventional employment. Some occupations can be carried out at home on a freelance basis, which may suit you better than doing the same work as an employee.

The advantage of starting off via a hobby is that you are doing the same thing that you have done for some time and feel confident about, with the added bonus that people are paying you for it. If you are thinking of doing this, you might benefit from some form of training, if you can afford the time and fees, to increase your knowledge, efficiency and skill.

Whatever you choose to do, it is important that it is something that is going to suit you. If you take up something unsuitable, for whatever reason, you are not going to like doing it; if you cannot manage to do it properly, your self-confidence will be undermined and this may prevent you from doing something else that you could do well.

A woman who has been running a home and looking after children should realise that she has gained experience in decision-making, leadership and organisation, which she can now make use of.

Look at yourself objectively and decide what you are capable of. Your state of health is obviously important: there is no point in taking up work which will prove too much for you physically. An activity which involves a lot of standing or heavy lifting and carrying may be too tiring for you; a lot of close work may prove a strain on middle-aged eyes; having to go out whatever the weather may be a health hazard to an older person. Do not take up anything that is obviously too demanding, with which you may not be able to cope.

It is no good taking up work where you have to deal mainly with figures if you are not really good at them, since figurework is unlikely to grow on you. If you are more interested in people, choose the type of work where you would have the chance to meet people and deal with them and their problems. Maybe you prefer practical to intellectual activity. How mobile are you? For some work, you must be able to go out occasionally, and may need a car.

How much time you have to spare or can squeeze out of the day for your work may be the crux of the decision on what you do. If you cannot work full-time without upsetting the family, you will have to find something that takes only part of your time. A mother with pre-school children will have to do her money-earning work in the evenings and at nights.

family and friends

You should discuss with your family what change your working at home is going to make in their lives. They may dislike the idea at first, but should know the reasons why you are doing it so that they can accept it without too much fuss.

Unless a husband or wife is in favour of the other spouse's working at home and is willing to give active support, things are going to be difficult. There are bound to be times when the other is going to have to do jobs he or she has not done in the past, as well as possibly giving some help needed in connection with the new work. Without support, it will be hard to work at home full-time, and even part-time could be complicated.

If you have elderly relatives or neighbours who depend on you in some way, you will have to explain to them that you are not going to be available as much as before, and that you will have to visit them at different times. Try not to let them feel neglected.

A major problem is dealing with casual visitors or social telephone calls during the hours that you have set aside for work. You need to be ruthless here, inviting them to call back at some other time when you can be free. It is no use thinking to yourself 'Oh, I'll make up the time later'—that time never comes, and you will have lost valuable working hours.

domestic duties

A housewife will have to organise her domestic life more carefully than before.

shopping and cooking
You may have to keep bigger stocks of food and household supplies and always have something in reserve so that you do not have to interrupt your work to slip round to the shop for forgotten items.

You should not waste your precious time going round the shops looking for bargains; it may be more economic to use the time for earning more money. You may have to restrict yourself to a few shops which you know have the range of goods you want at reasonable prices. Using the same shop(s) most of the time enables you to become familiar with the prices charged there so that when there are 'special offers', you will know whether they are good value.

You could write out your shopping list in the order in which you encounter the different items when walking round your local supermarket: this would make it easier for other people (the children, perhaps) who may not be used to that shop, to do your shopping for you.

Buying in larger quantities can save time, even though it means that you are spending a lot of your newly-earned money all at one go—on a dozen tins, say, of baked beans or of cat food. If you do not have the time or means of transport to go to a special shop which sells in bulk, you could buy large quantities of any item you regularly need when it is on special offer at your local supermarket. Some supermarkets also sell a range of groceries in catering packs or multiple packs.

Having a freezer saves on shopping time because you can buy quantities of frozen food and vegetables to put in your freezer for when you need them. Also, you can cook a batch of dishes in advance and store them away in the freezer; this saves on cooking time (and fuel costs).

If you are earning, you may be able to afford to have someone do some cooking for you in her home. Anyone tied to home who is a good cook may be glad of some extra money. Pay the proper rates. Commission fruit pies or cakes from one, say, and stews or meat loaf from another, and you will have home cooking and a well-fed family, grateful friends and neighbours—and more time to follow your money-earning activities, with a clear conscience.

housework and garden
Some people prefer the little-and-often technique of cleaning the house, others prefer a major purge once a week with everyone in the family doing a share. You may have to learn to be less perfectionist about the housework, and so will your family.

Where a man who had previously been out during the day now works at home, the woman who does the cleaning may have to rearrange the daily routine so as not to interfere with or distract him at work.

If you have not had many labour-saving appliances up to now, this may be the time to buy some. A good vacuum cleaner is going to get your carpets clean more quickly and efficiently than an old carpet sweeper. If you can afford a dishwasher, it may save much time and effort. An automatic washing machine, which carries out the whole washing process without any help from you, will save your time although initial capital expenditure can be high.

Clothes which do not require hand washing or ironing can save time and energy: check the information label on clothes, sheets, pillowcases and duvet covers before you buy, to find out whether you can machine-wash and drip-dry them.

The garden can be a distraction for someone working at home. Consider converting part of the garden into relatively trouble-free lawn and shrubs so as to cut down on work; the rest of the family should take their turn.

It is important that husband, wife and children realise that they should be prepared to accept specific responsibilities. They will have to be willing to do more for themselves—help in the house, go shopping, take more responsibility for their clothes, belongings, and so on. If, for instance, the children are made responsible for looking after their clothes and making their beds, they will have to learn that if they do not do so there will be only dirty clothes to wear and unmade beds to sleep in. Do not give in and do it yourself for the sake of peace and tidiness.

However well-meaning the rest of the family, it is likely that the mother will have to do a lot of overtime on the domestic front and even the best organised person will sometimes feel very tired.

Make sure you give yourself some time off—evenings or weekends and holidays. If earning money at home means ceaseless work, it will do you no good.

neighbours

Trouble with neighbours is obviously something you do not want. From the start, take particular care to tell them what you are doing and assure them that you will not bother them with your work as far as is possible. So, avoid noise at unrea-

sonable times—no one will want to hear you typing or machining at 2 am, even though you may have an urgent order to finish—and be particularly careful about visitors. People get annoyed by a constant stream of cars calling next door, parking in front of the wrong house, obstructing their entrance, callers shouting good-bye. To avoid friction here, ask your visitors and clients to cooperate and to avoid walking over bits of other people's gardens.

If you live in a block of flats or on a housing estate, anything that needs a lot of storage space may not be possible. Stocks of plastic materials would be a fire risk and so would flammable liquids such as adhesives and solvents.

Check that you are not in breach of any covenant in force on your house, be it rented or bought, as to what you may or may not do there. Look at your lease or the deeds of the house. If the title to the house is registered, an office copy of the register entries can be obtained from the Land Registry by completing form A44, available from HMSOs and law stationers shops; a search fee is payable. A specific restriction may have been imposed by agreement between neighbours or a general one by the land developer when a housing estate was being built or a landlord may have inserted one in the lease for a particular tenant or property. Not all covenants are enforceable and, in some circumstances, a relaxation may be permitted. Someone at the citizens advice bureau or a solicitor may help you to understand any obscure wording on a document.

Make sure that your building society or other mortgagee has no objections to your plans. When you applied for your mortgage, you probably said that the house was solely for your family's use as a residence. Most building societies would not object provided that any restrictive covenants were complied with, and any necessary planning permission was obtained.

PLANNING PERMISSION

If you want to add an extra room or convert a garage or put up an outbuilding, you may need to obtain planning permission as well as meeting the requirements of the Building Regulations (in Scotland, getting building control consent). If you are in doubt, ask the building inspector or planning officer of your local authority to let you know what, if anything, is necessary in your case.

You may have to get planning permission from the local authority to change the use of your premises, even if you own the house. For instance, strictly speaking, you need planning permission to use your garage to store goods, or if you want to undertake activities which are not incidental to the use of your house for domestic purposes—selling things from your house or using one room as a workroom, for instance. But there may be no point in involving the planning authority at the outset unless the neighbours are likely to complain. Small-scale business use may not count as change of use.

Whether permission is required or granted depends on the extent and type of the activity, whether you employ anyone else, whether it is likely to affect your neighbours. The local authority has discretion to allow or not allow according to its own criteria; if your application is refused, you have the right of appeal.

If you go ahead without the necessary approval, you may be fined and made to cease the activities and remove any buildings which are unauthorised.

If you do need (and get) planning permission for the new use of your premises, the planning department informs the rating authority who may notify the valuation officer. He may come to inspect the premises about reassessing the rateable value (or at least the part you are now using for your business). The rates you pay in the £ will go up from the lower domestic tariff to the commercial tariff for that part. At present, commercial ratepayers are not entitled to pay by instalments (but may be allowed to, on request).

INSURANCE

If you set up in business in your home, on however small a scale, you are technically speaking invalidating your normal householder's insurance policy. Most insurance policies involve signing a declaration which reads something on the lines of: 'I declare that . . .' and then there are a lot of statements, including one that says that the building is occupied '. . . solely by myself and my family and no business is carried on therein'. Also, the liability section of a householder's policy excludes any liability arising from the insured's trade, profession, business or employment. There is no shortcut round this by saying 'Well, I'm not actually the insured—my husband is, so of course this is different'. As far as the insurance company is concerned, it is not different. The householder's insurance applies jointly and severally and covers the deeds and misdeeds of the insured and family. So, if one of you, or even one of your children, is using the house for business, the whole of your policy is technically invalidated and the insurers would be entitled to refuse a claim on your policy, even if it arose from something domestic, nothing to do with the business activities.

For some activities carried on at home, and in respect of some professions—for instance, teaching, translating, typing—insurers will be willing (with some exclusions and perhaps a little extra premium) to go on covering the premises as though they were a private dwelling. However, a number of people coming in and out of your house on business could well affect your insurance cover for theft.

The insurers must be told if you are to use any part of the building for any other purposes than normal residence. What extra insurance cover you should take out depends on the type of work you do at home.

fire and burglary

When arranging a new policy, the insurers will be concerned about extra hazards regarding fire and burglary. It is quite likely that they will ask to survey the premises, and may then stipulate additional protection as far as burglary is concerned, such as window locks, secure locks on front and back doors, and in some circumstances a burglar alarm system.

Some business activities done from and in the home add nothing to the fire hazard. But if you are doing craftwork, such as lampshade making or woodwork, you may well have on the premises a larger quantity than normal of adhesives. In ordinary domestic quantities, these substances are fairly innocuous, but in larger quantities, used continuously in one room where the air could be quite heavy with their fumes, they become a genuine hazard: many modern adhesives can be easily ignited by a pilot light, a cigarette or an electric fire. There is a fire hazard in many plastic foams such as are used as filling for toys. Also, it can be dangerous to keep equipment on stairs or in passageways, impeding safe routes of escape.

Ask your insurers for advice on fire or burglary protection. Their advice is free and they are not going to report you to the local authority if it transpires that you are in breach of some bye-law or regulation—but they may refuse to insure you unless you comply. Similarly, the advice of the fire prevention officer of the county fire brigade is available free and so is advice from the crime prevention officer of the local police.

One point to be borne in mind when your work is at home is that if your home is damaged or destroyed, for whatever reason, you are also out of work. Your householder's policy helps to meet the cost of alternative accommodation for yourself and family while your home is being repaired. But it is most unlikely that you will be able to carry on your own business from the hotel or boarding house. To cover the extra expense of carrying on your money-earning activity elsewhere, you could take out loss-of-profits insurance—but check whether the cost of the premium is proportionate to your potential loss of earnings.

liability to others

For some work, public liability insurance is an essential. In the course of your activities, you may negligently cause injury to your customers or the public or damage to their property and an action may be brought against your for compensation. Public liability insurance would take care of compensation and costs awarded against you and also the costs involved in your defence. In practice, the insurers would take over the claim at the outset.

You may become involved in liability to your customers or others for injury or damage arising out of the sale or supply of defective or unsuitable goods. An extension to cater for this product liability can usually be obtained.

For some occupations, liability insurance can be quite difficult to obtain; you may have to consult an insurance broker. In a newly started business, the insurance company has only your word for it that you will be conscientious and careful.

You have to tell the insurers the nature of your work and what materials and equipment you are using; your premium will be calculated according to the risks involved.

Other people's property entrusted to you, for repair perhaps, is not covered by your householder's insurance for damage you may do to it, nor for its unexplained loss. But you may be able to take out special all-risks insurance for this.

You should get insurance for your liabilities when dealing with children, such as teaching them music or giving them extra tuition at home. All you may need to do is advise your insurers and get an extension to your existing householder's policy for this work.

If you employ another person in your home as part of a business you are running from your home—not as a housekeeper or similar sort of employment, which is in a different category—you have to make certain that if they do some damage to a client while working on your behalf, or by their negligence cause your client to have an accident, this can be covered by public liability insurance.

Where other people work in their own home for you, they must settle with their own insurers the effect on their house-holder's insurance. But you should inform your own insurers. For instance, you may need cover for your liability if you employ someone to pack goods for you, send them out unchecked, and a mistake in packing rendered the goods in some way dangerous or lethal.

lost in the post

If your work entails sending things away by post, this can cause problems if anything goes missing or arrives damaged. The post office has a compensation fee system for parcels, paying up to £200 in the event of loss or damage. Anything sent by first class letter post can be registered but this is fairly expensive and the compensation limits are £200, £400 and £600, depending on the fee paid. The post office has a free leaflet *How to send things you value through the post*.

For sending documents, plans, drawings, books, it may be worth asking your insurance company about ticket insurance, which is a form of all-risks insurance for documents in transit. However, it may be difficult when you first go into business because the insurers will want to know approximately how many parcels and of what value you are going to send during a year. There is a limit on the compensation paid per packet, and different ways of taking this insurance—it depends on the type of package and the business concerned. Claim settlement may be quicker than claiming from the post office. You do not always have to send the packages via the post office; ticket insurance can apply equally to rail or private carriers.

use of the car

Assuming that you are going to use your car or estate car in connection with your work, check in whose name the policy is. Anybody who is covered by the insurance—policyholder, named driver, or anyone driving with permission—may drive for social, domestic or pleasure purposes. A policy can be extended for use by the policyholder in person in connection with a business. But if the policyholder does not use the car for business purposes himself, the business use extension can be transferred without extra charge to another driver, provided that driver has the necessary clean driving and insurance record. But if the policyholder is using the car for business purposes, however little, this clause is, as it were, fully taken up and for another person also to use the car for business, an extra premium must be paid.

An ordinary policy for a private car specifically excludes commercial travelling, so you must be careful that you are not doing innocently what insurers and the law would call commercial travelling. As far as the motor insurance aspect goes, the line between commercial travelling and ordinary selling and delivering is a fine one. If you are doing even a little bit of using your car delivering or collecting orders, tell the insurers. Describe exactly what you are doing and the approximate volume of business done in that way. If this amounts to commercial travelling, the policy will cost more (but you and the family can use the car for social purposes under the same policy). Do not try to hide anything—if you are involved in an accident and are found to be carrying goods when you should not be, for instance, you will have been driving uninsured.

Where the car is being bought on hire purchase, strictly speaking if you are going to change the use of it, you ought to advise the hire purchase company.

If you want to use a trailer, you should have no problems about insuring it provided your driving licence is clear and your accident record is good and you have a suitable towing vehicle. The insurance for a trailer is more or less all-risks cover, depending on the desirability of the contents to thieves (nothing will keep a really determined thief out of a trailer). You may need to take out separate goods-in-transit insurance. Third party risks are covered by the motor policy of the towing vehicle while the two are attached to each other. It is sensible to insure a trailer where you insure the car, to make matters simpler if you should need to claim.

money

As your business begins to increase, so will the amount of money that you have to handle. Personal money in the house—husband's, wife's, children's—up to £100 can be covered under your householder's policy for an additional premium. However, for business money, a separate cash policy is necessary. For this, you have to give an estimate of the amount of money you take to the bank in any one week, or of the annual turnover.

Where large amounts of cash are kept on your premises, the house will be considered a target risk for break-ins. Your insurers will send round a surveyor and expect various precautions to be taken.

Often, when thieves break in for money, they damage the premises while getting in, and take other insured property as well. Even if you do not consider it worth insuring the money, the property you do insure will be placed at an additional risk, which may increase the premium that you have to pay for it. So, as soon as money comes in, bank it. You can arrange with your bank for night safe facilities after hours; there is no charge for this. When carrying any amounts of cash, avoid using the same route regularly.

personal insurance

The crucial question that insurers ask someone applying for any form of sickness insurance is 'What are your weekly earnings?'. When you start working for yourself, you are unlikely to have any idea of just how much you are going to earn. And without being able to answer this question, you are unlikely to get anything but cover for the minimum amounts.

Insurers may be reluctant about accepting you for any sickness insurance at all if you are starting to work freelance at home. Personal accident cover is less useful but easier to obtain. Even so, it has always been rather difficult in the case of people without a set income, such as housewives.

When you have become your family's breadwinner or joint breadwinner, or simply a more important person moneywise, it may be worth considering taking out a policy that will provide either a lump sum or an income for your dependants should you die. Traditionally, most life insurance is 'a policy on the husband's life to provide income for the widow on his death. But a husband may be rendered financially insecure by the death of his wife, and either can take out a policy on the other's life.

Some insurance companies offer pension schemes specifically directed towards the self-employed; for example, to provide a cash sum on 'retirement' and a monthly pension continuing for either spouse when the other dies.

national insurance

When you start being self-employed, you should notify your social security office.

Self-employed people are required to pay class 2 national insurance contributions. DHSS leaflet NI 41, available from social security offices, gives national insurance guidance for the self-employed.

It is possible to apply for exception from liability to pay class 2 national insurance contributions if your gross annual earnings are, or are likely to be, below a certain amount (£1050 in 1979/80). Before you apply, check whether being exempt will affect entitlement to any benefits, such as a retirement pension, you may have accrued from previous contributions. A married woman or a widow who has an existing right to reduced liability does not need to apply for exception on the grounds of small income. She is covered for retirement pension and sickness benefit by her husband's contributions. Leaflet NI 27A gives information about exception for people with small earnings from self-employment.

To pay class 2 contributions, either you get a card from the social security office on which to stick a stamp (bought at the post office) for each week, or you can arrange for direct debit of a bank or Girobank account.

Even when you pay class 2 contributions, you will not be entitled to claim unemployment benefit. To claim sickness benefit when self-employed, you need to produce some evidence of your normal earnings—your latest tax return will be useful for this. But you will not get an earnings-related supplement to augment the basic sickness payment.

In addition to the weekly class 2 contributions, a self-employed person becomes liable to an additional type of tax in the form of what is called a class 4 'contribution'. This is 5 per cent on annual profits or gains (not turnover) between certain amounts (£2250 and £7000 for 1979/80) and is collected by the Inland Revenue with schedule D income tax. It does not bring entitlement to any benefits. Leaflet NP 18, available from tax offices as well as social security offices, deals with class 4 contributions. There is also an Inland Revenue leaflet (IR 24) on the computation of profits for class 4 liability.

Your work from home may be in addition to an existing employment in which class 1 national insurance contributions are paid. If it is likely that the total of class 1 and class 2 contributions will exceed the maximum contribution payable under the national insurance regulations, you can apply for deferment of class 2 contributions in respect of the work done at home. This avoids unnecessary payments and refunds. Leaflet NP 28 *People with more than one job* can be obtained from local social security offices.

You may find that you are entitled to some state benefits because your income is low or you have dependants. The DHSS booklet FB2 *Which benefits?* tells you how you can get cash help. Supplementary benefit is paid only to someone who is available to work for an employer, which most self-employed people are not able or willing to be. However, if you have one or more children and can prove that you are working at least 30 hours a week, you can claim family income supplement (FIS) if your weekly takings are below the specified amount for your size of family. Leaflet FIS 1, available from post offices, gives details.

031- 225.
5774

WHAT TO CALL YOURSELF

If you decide to trade under your own name without any addition, you do not need to register it as a business name. But if you are using another name (Cuddly Toys of Milton Keynes, for example) or your own name with an addition (Jeremy Fish and Sons, for example) or if you are a married woman using her maiden name, you must register the name with the appropriate registrar of business names. The registry for England or Wales is at Pembroke House, 40–56 City Road, London EC1Y 2DN; for Scotland at 102 George Street, Edinburgh EH2 3DJ; for Northern Ireland at 43–47 Chichester Street, Belfast BT1 4RJ.

The registry will send you on request the Department of Trade's pamphlet *Notes for guidance on registration of business names.* This includes the warning that registration as such does not give sole rights to a name nor protection against someone else using the same name or you unwittingly using someone else's. The pamphlet also warns that the registrar does not consult the trade marks index when considering applications for a proposed new business name and the acceptance of a particular name is not an indication that no trade mark rights exist in it.

You cannot register any name you like. If you want to use a name including the words 'royal' or 'queen', for instance, or if the name would imply that the business is larger or more comprehensive than it is—'World Wide Toys', for example—that name would probably not be allowed.

For registration of a name by an individual, you need to complete form RBN1 (there is a different form for a company or partnership) and pay a registration fee of £1. If accepted, you are issued with a certificate of registration to be put up in a conspicuous position at your principal place of business. Do not go to the expense of having stationery printed or signs made up with a business name, or a business entry in the telephone directory, until you know from the registry that the name is acceptable.

registering a trade mark

In addition to having your own business name, you may want to have a distinctive sign to identify your products. To protect any symbol, design or word that you choose, you can register it as a trade mark at the Trade Marks Registry. This entitles you to the exclusive right to use the mark in relation to the goods for which it is registered. Before doing so, it would be wise to check at the registry that a similar mark has not already been registered: a search in person costs 35p for each quarter of an hour in the search room; by post, £12.50 per search and you normally have to wait about six weeks for the result.

The registrar will advise (fee £3.50) on the distinctiveness of a proposed mark: some devices and words are not allowed.

The fee for lodging an application is £23, with a further fee of £34.50 when the mark is registered. If you want to use a name mark separate from a symbol, it is advisable to make a separate application for each as well as one for the combination.

Before registration, the mark has to be advertised in the *Trade Marks Journal,* and time allowed for anyone to oppose it. Registration is initially for a period of seven years and can be renewed at fourteen year intervals after that.

Application forms and a free pamphlet about applying for a trade mark are available from the Trade Marks Registry, The Patent Office, 25 Southampton Buildings, London WC2A 1AY.

GETTING YOUR WORK

Start promoting yourself in a small way by advertising on newsagents' window boards and in the local paper(s). In some localities, there is an advertising paper which is distributed free to every house and this often brings good results.

You can take a few lines in the personal or classified column or invest in a semi-display advertisement. Repeat at intervals if you want to keep your name before the public. If you take a standing advertisement (that is, one that is repeated every day or week, preferably on the same page of the paper), you will get a discount. It may be wiser not to book a very long run in case the first adverts generate a lot of enquiries.

It depends on what kind of service you are selling, but advertising outside your area may involve travelling to deliver your products, and consequently time and expense, and this could make the difference between profit and loss.

For some occupations, there are specialist magazines, and it may be worth investing in a few advertisements in an appropriate one. Consult the classified index in the annual *Willing's Press Guide*, in the public reference library, to find out what magazines, journals, newsletters and other publications there are; current advertising rates are given in *British Rate and Data* (monthly), which also should be in the library.

Some public libraries keep lists of people prepared to do certain jobs—the names of translators and interpreters, for instance. It costs nothing to have your name on the list.

It may be a good idea to have cards describing your services:

Jane A Smith

20 High Street
Newtown

telephone: Newtown 610

Dressmaking, alterations and repairs
Wedding dresses a speciality

You may be able to make a handbill advertisement yourself by using stick-on lettering or typing it and getting it photocopied or duplicated:

RUSSIAN, SWEDISH AND GERMAN TRANSLATIONS

Qualified translator prepared to translate both technical reports and business correspondence. Work will be done promptly and typed efficiently.

Peter Hardy
'The Knoll'
Oak Tree Lane
Little Wallington   telephone: Blasted Heath 317

Distribute your cards or advertisements to people and firms in your area who you think might be interested.

Placing a notice or sign outside your house may require consent from your local authority; ask at the planning department.

If what you do is unusual (canary-boarding or sail-mending, say) send a note with details (and perhaps a photograph) to the features editor of the local newspaper, or to the local radio station. It is always worth contacting local papers: they have to have something to write about, and a new venture of almost any sort is news—locally, that is. Editorial mention is free publicity and can bring in a lot of business.

Offer to visit local groups (mainly women's) to talk about what you do. Many groups are on the lookout for speakers for an evening or afternoon, to fill their calendar of events. Generally, they pay the speaker's expenses. Take examples of your work and a handout with your name and address.

the telephone

The telephone is likely to become an essential factor in your activities. You may want to put an extension into the room you are using for work: this will cost you an initial £8 for the connection and then an additional £1.60 on your quarterly rental. An alternative is to convert your telephone to a 'plan 4' system, with plug-in sockets so that you can move the instrument from one room to another. (Post office leaflet DLA 100 gives details.) The installation charge is £8 for two sockets and £8 for any further sockets; the additional rental charge is £1.10 a quarter for two sockets, plus 25p for any further sockets. Additional quarterly rental charges are higher for a business line.

If you become established enough to justify the outlay, you can have a separate business line brought into the house, with a different number and listing in the telephone directory. A business line entitles you to an entry, free of charge, in the yellow pages under the classification of your choice (as well as the normal entry in the white alphabetical pages) of the local telephone directory. In addition, you can pay for a semi-display advertisement in the yellow pages. The quarterly rental for a business line is £9.75; ask your telephone area office what the connection charge would be—it can be as much as £45.

Post office leaflet DLX 4 lists charges for telephone services and apparatus; value added tax is charged in addition.

Ensure that you have an up-to-date dialling code book (free from your telephone area office) and all the directories you are likely to need—some extra directories are free.

It is worth taking trouble to develop a good telephone manner. Be pleasant and friendly, but businesslike and firm at the same time. Try not to get involved in long-drawn-out conversations— this is a waste of your (by now valuable) time, and means that the line is blocked for other callers. Have a list or memorise the salient facts you need to know or to give an enquirer, be clear about your charges and conditions, about arrangements for collection or delivery, about timing and special requirements.

Keep a calendar or desk diary beside the telephone, and never fail to put down an order or appointment as soon as it is made. Train other members of your household, who may answer the telephone when you are out or busy, to do likewise and to be accurate and reliable over taking and giving messages. Make sure there is always a pad and pencil beside the telephone.

If you have to make telephone calls which are likely to be lengthy or are outside your local area, try to time them so that you take advantage of the cheaper rates: after 6 pm (cheapest) or between 8 and 9 in the morning or between 1 and 6 pm.

There are answering sets on which you can pre-record a message for callers in your absence. If you use one, record your message pleasantly and humanly so as not to put off callers. Post office leaflet DLE 520 describes the sets the post office provides: connection charge is £5, quarterly rental £9 or (for a longer message) £18. Other answering machines and those that record messages from callers can be hired from private commercial firms.

There are also facilities for incoming calls to be transferred to another number via interception by the operator or, for calls on the same exchange, by a special switch system on the telephone. Post office leaflet DLB 200 describes subscriber controlled transfer of telephone calls.

Selling your work

It is important to know how to sell what you have to offer. This may be by working to specific orders only, so that once you have been asked to do something, the product has a buyer waiting for it.

You may get orders either direct by promoting yourself, or through some form of middleman (such as a shop, gallery, agent). Similarly, if you produce things on spec, you can sell them either via a middleman or direct.

When you do it via a middleman, an individual agent or a shopkeeper sells what you have made, either buying outright from you or selling for you on commission, perhaps on a sale-or-return basis.

An advantage of selling via an agent or middleman is that you do not need to use up time and energy in looking for individual outlets and will benefit from the agent's contacts and experience. However, you may not be allowed or able to set the price and the agent will take a commission. The workflow is out of your control and may be spasmodic and the agent may suddenly withdraw. If you are successful, you may be under pressure to produce in quantity, and to meet deadlines not of your own choosing.

When selling direct to the client, you are in charge of the whole operation and can do it in your own time and way. But it is time-consuming and you may get the pricing wrong until you are experienced. You may need a car or some other form of transport to get to, say, a local market.

If the customer comes to your home, you do not waste time and energy in travelling and can assess his needs individually. However, you may have to organise appointments, and visits may be time-consuming and interruptive. Not only do you have to have a suitable room, but also to keep the whole place reasonably tidy. Neighbours may not like the comings and goings, and you may find that you need planning permission for this use.

trades unions
With some activities, it may be difficult to place your work if you are not a member of the relevant trades union. (Conversely, some unions do not accept someone for membership who is not already active in the particular trade. And a few unions do not accept people who are self-employed or freelance.) For instance, for illustrative or photographic work, the Society of Lithographic Artists, Designers, Engravers and Process Workers (SLADE) or the National Union of Journalists or the National Graphical Association would be the relevant unions; for writing, the National Union of Journalists or the Writers' Guild of

Great Britain; for printing, the Society of Graphical and Allied Trades, the National Graphical Association, SLADE, or the National Society of Operative Printers, Graphical and Media Personnel (NatSOPA). To get machine knitting work at home, you may need to join the National Union of Hosiery and Knitwear Workers, and for dressmaking or repair work, the National Union of Tailors and Garment Makers. Overall, the National Union of General and Municipal Workers is concerned about people who work at home. Any union takes protective action on behalf of its members where there are difficulties over payment, conditions of work, contracts, statutory requirements, legal problems.

Information about the various unions, and head office addresses, are obtainable from the Trades Union Congress (organisation and industrial relations department, Congress House, Great Russell Street, London WC1B 3LS). Most unions have branch offices for each area of the country, and you may be able to get in touch direct with the appropriate branch through your local telephone directory.

Getting supplies

If you are extending a hobby or spare-time interest, you are likely to have at least the basic necessary equipment, and experience in using it. You may have to buy more, larger, better, more versatile, more efficient versions, or extras.

Where it is up to you to provide the raw materials, make use of any bulk or wholesale supplies available. You may qualify for trade discount and be able to buy at restricted cash-and-carry stores.

A cash-and-carry store sells items at wholesale prices, in bulk, to bona fide traders (some also allow members of the public to buy direct). Find out whether there is one near you for the goods you need (look in the yellow pages: 'C' for cash and carry, or 'W' for warehouse) and telephone to ask what are the terms for traders. Some warehouses require evidence in support of your claim to be a trader, in the form of headed stationery or printed card, invoices with your business name, VAT registration number, bank or other references. You may be issued with a card to present whenever you go to buy, to prove your credentials as a trader.

Try to establish a good relationship with a reliable supplier (or two) so that you do not have to fail on a job because a supplier has let you down or there is an unaccountable delay in getting delivery of an essential material or ingredient (sugar or paper or upholstery tacks). Keep a close watch on your stocks and check regularly to see whether anything vital is running low.

COSTING YOUR WORK

One of the most difficult points for someone who has not previously worked on his or her own, or asked for payment for any product or service provided, is to know how much to charge. Even if you have previously done the same thing in the role of an employee (a typist or hairdresser, for example), it is not easy to assess what your work has really cost. There are many elements to bear in mind.

Look at your method of working, stage by stage, and check what you put into it in the way of actual materials (specially bought and from stock), incidentals, overheads, time; add a figure for clear profit.

time

To work out the financial loss or gain of an hour spent on a task, as well as the time spent in doing the actual work you should be costing in the time taken up by promoting yourself, getting the order for that particular job, any paperwork involved, and perhaps delivery of the finished goods. Until you have done enough to realise how much you can make in an hour of your time, it is probably impossible to set an hourly rate for yourself.

If your customers do not come and collect from you, delivering the goods can prove quite expensive, in terms of your time as well as petrol or fares. It may not be acceptable to charge for this as a separate item, so you must incorporate an approximate amount for cost of delivery.

overheads

Another element difficult to disentangle will be your overheads: lighting and heating the room(s) you use, the higher rates you may be paying on that part of your premises, the telephone rental and, with machine work, the electricity consumed. You may also be using storage space—in garage or attic or cellar or garden shed—which would otherwise be utilised differently by you or your household, but this 'loss' is almost impossible to translate into financial terms. With some jobs, special cleaning of the workroom or equipment may be required, or maintenance of a machine, and this expense ought to be taken into account, too.

You may have to build an allowance for bad debts into your costing structure, and remember to allow for the fact that you may not be paid until some time after you send in a bill.

equipment

The cost of the extra equipment you buy should be covered, and also its depreciation. To work out depreciation approximately, you should estimate how long you expect to be able to use the article and how much you may be able to get for it when you come to sell. Deduct the selling figure from the buying cost and divide the difference by the number of years of anticipated use. Supposing the price you pay is £150, the estimated life is 5 years, and the resale price then £60:

$$\begin{array}{r} £150 \\ -\ 60 \\ \hline \end{array}$$

$$90 \div 5 = £18 \text{ p.a.}$$

Also, you should allow for loss on capital. If instead of using the money for buying the equipment, you had invested the lump sum at, say, 7 per cent, you have to add the notional loss of interest in your costing: in this case, £10.50 p.a. (If you had to borrow money to buy the equipment, the interest charged is not a notional but an actual cost.) Therefore, you should recover through your charges in each year £28.50 spread over each working day or working hour.

Paperwork of some extent is almost unavoidable. As well as the amount of your time spent on it, you should keep a note of the paper and envelopes you use for letters and accounts, the stamps, packaging materials, files and other office stationery (erasers, staplers, clips, glue, writing implements, batteries for calculator). In some cases, there may be a specific outlay on a particular job (telephone calls, for instance, or a series of letters), but in others you will have to assume a total figure and spread it out to add a fraction to your overall charge per job. This may be difficult to calculate until you know how many jobs you are going to get through in a month or year.

When the work involves making something, it should not be too difficult to work out how much you have spent on the materials or ingredients. If you have bought your supplies in bulk, you will have to break down the total outlay into smaller units (per half lb from your 10 lb bag, perhaps) for charging to each job. Even apparently minor items, such as thread, string, nails, adhesive, mount up into an accountable factor. With some work, you have to buy the materials some time before you are going to use or be able to charge for them, and this capital loss should, strictly, be allowed for.

estimating and reviewing

You may have to give an estimate when given an order and then charge specifically after you have completed the job. Until you have had some experience of the costs involved, try not to estimate too precisely because it will be difficult to be accurate enough to be fair to yourself or to your customer. Give an approximate range of the likely cost, making it clear that the final figure may vary upwards or downwards. Once a firm quotation is accepted, you are bound by it.

Find out what professionals in the same line of business are charging and compare this with what you would have to charge for such work to make your venture profitable. You can then uprate or downrate yourself according to the circumstances. This applies especially to a service or skill that does not end up in a visible product: for example, being a consultant or an agent, a teacher or researcher, a repairer or hirer, a minder or landlady. As a general rule, people employing your services will have a fair idea of the going rate, and that may determine what you can charge.

Do not knowingly undercharge, even to begin with when you may be feeling unconfident about your abilities. It may create ill feeling and loss of custom if you then suddenly increase your charges sharply for the next or subsequent orders.

It is important to keep a steady eye on your outgoings and incomings, to make sure that there is a reasonable balance between the two and that you are not subsidising your customers by mistake. The real state of your financial affairs will not emerge for some months, or even years, but you should check the position regularly—monthly, or even weekly.

DEALING WITH CUSTOMERS

An essential principle is to meet all deadlines: if you allow yourself to fail to deliver on the appointed date (or even hour), you will never make a success of your venture. Try to be firm when asked to do a rush job and do not accept if it means falling behind with another job to which you are already committed. Ideally, you should establish a steady workflow, but this is unlikely to be possible in practice and there are bound to be emergencies and unforeseen delays or difficulties.

Whenever feasible, allow a 'fail safe' period in your timetable for each job, so that if there is a power cut, a machine breakdown, a family crisis, you have time in hand to catch up. Remember that 'flu or a heavy cold in winter could throw you out of action for up to a week.

And since you are your own best asset, do not exhaust yourself and your abilities by overwork: your timetable must include days off and a holiday (or two). The flexibility of freelance work is one of its attractions, but can be a hazard if it leads you to abuse your own resources.

charging

You may find it difficult and embarrassing at first to look someone in the eye (particularly a friend) and say 'That will cost you £xx, please'. But the firmer and more clearcut you can be over the transaction, the less awkward it will be. It is no good being diffident or apologetic—this may even make the other person doubt your ability, and your price.

It is generally better to stick to the charge or scale you have decided to adopt, regardless of who the customer is. It will bring accounting complications if you vary according to the recipient for each job, and may well arouse ill will and lead eventually to loss of custom.

It is likely that it will be up to you to introduce the subject of payment. Do so as early as is tactful in the proceedings, so that there is no misunderstanding or waste of time over whether the customer can afford what you are offering. Make sure that people know what your charges are when they telephone, even if they do not ask. It is generally a good idea to confirm in writing.

Specify clearly what you are charging for, including materials where appropriate. There may be items which your customer will see as 'hidden extras' but which you consider obvious expenses: pills for the cat you are boarding, for instance, or tacks and braid for an upholstery job, or the ream of paper for typing a thesis. If the stationery or whatever you need is not provided, buy it and get a receipt to attach to the bill so that the client can see exactly what he is paying for over and above the actual work.

Where your costs vary according to the season (in cooking perhaps because the ingredients are seasonal), you have to decide whether to vary your prices, too, or spread the higher costs over the whole year.

If you have established a scale of charges—for example, for photographic work, bed and breakfast, hairdressing, kennelling—have it printed or typed for customers to look at.

When the time comes for payment, be businesslike about presenting your bill: preferably, have it written out (or typed) and ready for your customer when the work is delivered or collected. Keep a copy. Unless you have headed stationery, make sure that your name and address appear on the bill; also, your telephone number (for repeat orders).

Always keep a record of what you have been paid, for what, by whom and how, particularly if it is a cash transaction. It may be tempting just to pocket the notes without showing their receipt in your accounts, but you will end up with tax queries as well as accountancy problems if you do this.

Bills that you send to the customer, rather than hand over for immediate payment, should state clearly that you require payment within, say, three weeks. Offering a discount for prompt payment may be an incentive, but you must allow for this in your costing.

Where the job is a long-drawn-out one or is being done in stages, you should arrange for part-payment, in advance or at an intermediate stage, otherwise you will be out of pocket for too long. You may run into 'cash flow' problems (that is, lack of ready money available), especially if you have had to pay out for materials or another person's work long before you get paid yourself. You may need to ask for an advance of cash in order to buy materials that you do not have in stock. Some firms settle their invoices only once a quarter; if you get an order from a large firm, ask about their timing of payments.

bad payers

There will inevitably be a number of bad debts which have to be written off. Do not send more than one stamped reminder—if subsequent ones go unstamped, there is hope that the debtor will take notice.

Keep a black list, 'and refuse to do further work for a debtor, at least not until the previous account is settled or unless payment is made in advance. Where possible, alert others who may have dealings with the person. If the work came via an advertisement, notify the publication concerned: they may be able to apply pressure on your behalf or at least warn others. It is seldom worth employing a debt-collecting organisation, but if you are willing to spend a few pounds on a county court summons, this may lead to sudden payment by the debtor.

Bad debts can be shown as a loss on a tax return. The *Money Which? Tax-Saving Guide* (March 1979) explains how to present debts on a tax return.

It is unlikely that anyone paying you personally for work you have done in your home will try to pass off a dud cheque on you, but have no compunction about asking to see a cheque card. Compare the signatures and write the card number yourself on the back of the cheque in case you need to invoke the bank's guarantee. If you are in any doubt about a customer's financial integrity or standing, or if he or she is a total stranger to you, do not accept a cheque for any amount over the £50 limit guaranteed by the card: insist on cash instead. Even a dud cheque, however, should not be thrown away because it is evidence of an agreed debt.

If the work you do involves having other people's possessions left with you while you work on them or for repair (a picture to frame, a chair to re-upholster, a clock to mend) give a ticket to make sure that the right thing will be collected by or on behalf of the right person. Be sure always to have the owner's or deliverer's name and address, or at least a telephone number, in case no one comes to collect at the appointed time. By law, under the Torts (Interference with Goods) Act 1977, you have to try to contact the owner or responsible person, but after making reasonable efforts to obtain instructions about the uncollected goods, you have the right to sell or dispose of an abandoned item. Before selling, however, you have to send in writing, by registered or recorded delivery post, due notice (in cases where money is owed, not less than three months) of the date on or after which you propose to sell. If large amounts are involved, get legal advice first.

KEEPING ACCOUNTS

You should keep a careful record of all financial transactions concerned with your work. This is important not only to check whether you are making a profit or loss but also because of legal requirements either now or later.

As soon as you start to earn or pay out any money at all, keep a record of all expenses and payments as they arise. Make sure that the full date is on everything. Fill in cheque stubs and paying-in slips clearly and fully.

A simple ruled cash book may be enough to start with: you can enter what you have earned at one side and at the other enter expenses, with dates and any other relevant details. Keep distinct records of cash and banking transactions. All money received (cash and cheques) must be paid in, even if you then withdraw it again.

What records need to be kept will be dictated by the volume of work involved. For instance, a writer whose year's work produces, say, one book may have just a single receipt of cash from the publisher with few expenses—perhaps paper, type-writer ribbons, postage, fares. On the other hand, someone doing hairdressing will have lots of regular small receipts of cash and numerous payments for stock, equipment, telephone, and would need a more elaborate cash book for payments, VAT records, and so on.

It is wise to write up your account books at least once a week.

Where applicable, the following should be recorded, with dates:

* payments made for stock
* payments made for other purchases or services
* money received and from whom
* goods or services supplied and to whom
* cash drawn for personal use

Although records can be simple, they must be comprehensive and capable of providing information for income tax purposes or for value added tax (or, if VAT registration is not yet required, capable of being adapted later to provide the necessary information).

If you decide that more elaborate records are necessary, go to a stationer's or office equipment shop and examine what cash record books and account books are available. A loose-leaf analysis book with, say, 4 columns for receipts and 16 columns for payments enables you to keep a cumulative check on how your venture is proceeding (with a cross-check for arithmetical accuracy) and also provides the figures you may need for submission to bank manager, accountant, Inland Revenue, Customs and Excise.

You must keep all invoices, bills, copies of receipts given, cheque stubs, letters, and anything else at all relating to your takings and expenditure. File them in date order. If not many, they can be put into a folder or box file or on a spike; or keep them in a ring binder, numbered and cross-referenced to your account books. It is a good idea to separate the papers for each accounting year so that when you come to make your declaration of income for tax purposes, you will have all the relevant material to hand and will not have to go ferreting amongst old bills and letters to find out how much you earned in a preceding year. Keep everything for at least three years—six years, to be on the safe side. The Inland Revenue (and Customs and Excise for VAT) have the right to examine your records at any time and you are obliged to produce relevant information on demand.

Always make a note of any item that might possibly be allowable for tax purposes. It is difficult to get a claim for any items allowed if they have not been recorded in the business books.

Be especially careful to record all expenses that relate to your work where part of your business expenses come out of the household account, such as electricity or telephone bills. You will need some record of all such expenses when compiling a claim for tax allowances.

The money that comes in and goes out for your work should be kept strictly separate from your personal and household finances. Have two cheque books and paying-in books, using one of each for business and one for private payments. Or you could open a separate bank or Girobank account, in the business name if you have one. But some banks charge for each transaction until or unless you keep in your current account more than the bank's minimum for charging. It is essential to get a statement at regular intervals so that you can check whether the balance agrees with your account books.

To make the money work for you while you are not using it, you could put your takings into a deposit account, a building society or the national savings bank. It is sensible to set aside in a savings account some money to meet tax and VAT liabilities as and when these fall due.

having an accountant

It could be worthwhile to get an accountant to advise and help you on the best method of keeping proper accounts and how to claim any expenses allowable against tax for the self-employed.

If you know an accountant or book-keeper who is working at or from home, ask for his or her help with your accounts—paying the appropriate fee for this professional service. A book-keeper can show you how to keep your accounts, an accountant may be able to help also with advice on some other aspects of your financial affairs.

If you do not know of a particular accountant, the bank manager may be able to suggest someone. But try to find out whether the accountant you know or have been told about is experienced in the kind of accounting or tax work your venture entails. Or you can write to the Institute of Chartered Accountants (in England and Wales: PO BOX 433, Moorgate Place, London EC2P 2BJ; Scotland: 27 Queen Street, Edinburgh EH2 1LA) and ask for the address of the nearest district society to get the names of qualified chartered accountants in your area. The Association of Certified Accountants (29 Lincoln's Inn Fields, London WC2A 3EE) also has members throughout the country. The names of accountants who are members of the British Association of Accountants and Auditors (Stamford House, 2 Chiswick High Road, London W4 1SU) are listed in the Association's yearbook, available in public libraries.

When first contacting a firm of accountants, make it clear that you need somebody who knows about the financial aspects of a self-employed or freelance person. An accountant knowledgeable about the hazards and complexities of self-employment can save you a lot of money as well as time; one who specialises in a different area could be unaware of all the pitfalls and possibilities.

Professional accountants charge on an hourly basis, according to seniority and type of work (ranging from about £8 to £40 an hour, plus expenses, but there is no fixed scale). Specify (preferably in writing) what work you want an accountant to do for you and ask what his charge is likely to be. His bill should be itemised according to the work you have agreed between you—for example, giving advice, preparing tax return, dealing with value added tax, any other book-keeping matters.

the accounting year
With the possible exception of the first year, your accounts should run for a 12-month period which begins and ends on the same date each year. But your accounting year need not necessarily be the calendar year 1 January to 31 December nor need it coincide with the tax year (6 April to 5 April).

Because of the way in which self-employed tax assessments are made, substantial tax advantages or disadvantages can result from the selection of the annual accounting date, particularly if the business is seasonal. Generally speaking, choose a date for the beginning of the first accounting period that gives greater emphasis on low rather than high earning periods. For example, if the high period was during the summer months, it would probably be better to choose the end of May as the annual accounting date; if the business started in January, the first accounts would then cover a period of 17 months; if the business started in September, the first accounts would cover the 10-month period to the end of May. But if the business started in May, it would normally be unwise to select a date beyond the following May because this would result in two high periods being included in the calculations as the basis for the first three years' tax assessments.

TAX

The *Money Which? Tax-Saving Guide*, published in March each year, deals with tax if you are self-employed or do any freelance work (see particularly the March 1979 issue). The Inland Revenue has a free pamphlet *Starting in business* (IR28 available at tax offices and from Somerset House, London WC2R 1LB), which gives an outline of how tax is assessed on profits, what records should be kept, allowable expenses, payment of tax, and includes advice about VAT and national insurance. In it there is a copy of form 41G which you should use to notify your local inspector of taxes (listed in the telephone directory under Inland Revenue) as soon as you start to work on your own.

Annual accounts will have to be submitted to the tax inspector, giving details of your trading profit. The accounts need not necessarily be professionally prepared but they must be clearly set out and accurate. (The local tax office can be asked for advice about preparing accounts for your tax return.) If you do decide to use an accountant, he will not only do the accounts but also will negotiate with the taxman on your behalf.

If you are genuinely self-employed, you will be taxed under schedule D. This allows you to claim tax relief on more expenses than if you work for an employer and are taxed by PAYE under schedule E. To be considered self-employed, you have to prove to the taxman's satisfaction that no one person has sole rights to your working time. Therefore, try to get work from several sources and pay your own national insurance stamp. If you supply a service to only one, or predominantly to one customer, a formal letter or contract might clarify your position as an independent, self-employed contractor.

tax in the first years
If you do isolated freelance or spare-time work, you will be taxed on the profit you make in the current tax year (6 April to 5 April). The tax may be collected through the PAYE system if you are also an employed person.

If your self-employed activities are a proper business, adding up to more than occasional freelance work, you will normally be taxed on what is called a preceding year basis: a tax bill for the 1979/80 tax year, for example, will be based on the profit made in the accounting year which ended during the 1978/79 tax year. For the first years of the business, there are special rules for assessing the tax due, based on the first or immediately preceding 12 months, depending on when the end of your accounting period falls (leaflet IR28 gives details, with examples).

Since the profits of the first 12 months in business are used in calculating three years' assessments, it is best to keep them as low as possible. With some activities, the profits vary according to the time of year: the best earning period may be just before Christmas, or more work might be done in the summer than in the winter. If your accounting year starts just before the 'best time' (which in the first year is not likely to be very profitable anyway), the second 'best time' is not included in the first year's trading. There are various tunes that can be played using the opening bases of assessment; since the starting date and the date of the first accounts can be significant, it would be wise to consult an accountant (if that is the intention) before any irrevocable decisions have been taken.

There are also special rules for the tax years immediately preceding the date when a business ceases.

wife's earnings

Even where a wife is earning money for herself by working freelance or running a business on her own, it is her husband who normally has to pay the tax due on her profits (claiming wife's earned income allowance as well as married man's personal allowance). A husband and wife can choose to have the wife's earned income taxed separately, instead of the wife's earnings being aggregated with her husband's income for tax. But this is an advantage only for a couple who are in a high-rate tax category. The application to be taxed separately has to be made jointly, not earlier than six months before or not later than twelve months after the relevant tax year; the wife's earnings will continue to be taxed separately until a joint notice of withdrawal is given. Leaflet IR13 deals with *A wife's earnings election.*

allowable business expenses

Certain expenses you incur in the course of your work can be deducted from your takings to arrive at the amount of your income liable for tax.

The sort of expenses you can claim for are the materials needed for your work, heating and lighting the room you work in, the telephone, travel in connection with your work, clothes outside your normal requirements, specialist books or magazines, and the premiums for insurance relating wholly to your business.

However, when you have been claiming tax relief on rates or rent for using part of your home exclusively for business, should you later sell it, you do not get exemption from capital gains tax on that part of the residence for which you have been claiming. If, for instance, you had a five-roomed house and claimed tax relief for one room of it where you worked, one-fifth of any profit on selling the house would be subject to CGT. It would be wiser to restrict a tax claim to such items as use of telephone or electricity, and to avoid claiming that any room or rooms are used exclusively for your work. A leaflet (CGT 8) on capital gains tax is available free from tax offices.

Although the rules for deducting an item as a business expense are that it is 'wholly and exclusively for the purposes of the trade' you can, in many cases, obtain the Inland Revenue's agreement to a claim for a proportion of expenditure for something you use partly for business and partly for private purposes. This is quite specifically a concession and not an entitlement as of right—but claim, and be prepared to agree to a disallowance. If claiming part of the cost of your car as a business expense, keep a mileage record distinguishing between business and personal use so that you can extricate the business percentage for your tax claim.

The table on the next page, taken from *Money Which?* March 1979, summarises what is normally allowed and not allowed by Inland Revenue as a business expense.

BUSINESS EXPENSES

	NORMALLY ALLOWED	NOT ALLOWED
Basic costs and general running expenses	Cost of goods bought for resale and raw materials used in business. Advertising. Delivery charges. Heating. Lighting. Rates. Telephone. Replacement of small tools and special clothing. Postage. Stationery. Subscriptions. Accountant's fees. Bank charges on business accounts.	Initial cost of machinery, vehicles, equipment, permanent advertising signs (but may qualify as capital allowance). Buildings. Expenses incurred before initial launching of business.
Use of home for work	Proportion of telephone, lighting, heating, cleaning and insurance. Proportion of rent and rates, if use part of home *exclusively* for business—but claiming these may mean some capital gains tax to pay if you sell your home.	
Wages and salaries	Payments to employees or outworkers. Reasonable pay for wife or husband provided actually employed.	Your own wages or salary, or that of any partner.
Taxes and national insurance	Employer's national insurance contributions for employees. VAT on allowable business expenses if not a registered trader for VAT (and, in certain circumstances, even if you are).	Income tax. Capital gains tax. Capital transfer tax. Your own national insurance contributions.

	NORMALLY ALLOWED	NOT ALLOWED
Entertaining	Reasonable entertainment of overseas trade customers and their overseas agents (and normally your own costs on such an occasion).	Any other business entertaining—eg entertainment of UK customers.
Gifts	If to advertise your business (or things it sells), gifts costing up to £2 a year to each person. Gifts (whatever their value) to employees.	Food, drink, tobacco, or vouchers for goods given to anyone other than employees.
Travelling	Hotel and travel expenses on business trips. Travel between different places of work. Running costs of own car: whole of cost if used wholly for business, proportion if used privately as well.	Cost of buying a car or van (but may qualify as capital allowance).
Interest payments	Interest on overdrafts and loans for business purposes.	Interest on capital paid or credited to partners. Interest on overdue tax.
Hire purchase	Hire charge part of payments (ie the amount you pay *less* the cash price).	Cash price of what you are buying on hire purchase (but may qualify as capital allowance).
Hiring	Reasonable charge for hire of capital goods, including car.	
Insurance	Business insurance—eg public liability, fire and theft, motor, for employees.	Your own life or health insurance.
Trade marks	Fees paid to register trade mark or design.	
Legal costs	Costs of recovering debts; defending business rights; preparing service agreements; appealing against rates.	Expenses (including stamp duty) for acquiring land and buildings. Fines and other penalties for breaking the law.
Repairs	Normal repairs and maintenance.	Cost of additions, alterations or improvements.

A self-employed person who is paying into an 'approved' personal pension or retirement annuity scheme can claim relief at his top rate of tax for the premiums being paid, provided these are under 15 per cent of non-pensionable earnings and not more than £3000 per annum.

If in doubt about any expense, claim. It is better for a claim to be disallowed by the tax inspector than not to try—you will not be told by Inland Revenue if you have omitted to claim for a permissible item.

capital allowances and stock relief

The cost of buying equipment or machinery—a typewriter, sewing machine, calculator, photocopier, kiln—is not an allowable business expense, but you can make a deduction, called a capital allowance, for such a capital asset if used for the purposes of the trade. The allowance you can claim can be up to 100 per cent of the cost for the accounting year in which you bought the item; if you claim less than 100 per cent, you can claim further capital allowances in future years.

To allow for the effect of inflation on the value of your stock during the year, a proportion of the appreciated value (if more than 10 per cent of your taxable profit less capital allowances) can be deducted from your taxable profit.

the tax you pay

The law requires a taxpayer to notify the Inland Revenue of any new source of income within 12 months of the end of the tax year in which the income first arose, even if the inspector of taxes has not sent a tax return for completion, and irrespective of whether there is a profit or loss, and even if you do not yet have all the figures. The onus of notifying is specifically on the taxpayer and failure to do so can lead to penalties and payment of interest on arrears.

Your profit counts as your earned income and you are liable for tax on it in the same way as an employed person is on his salary and you pay at the same rates as anyone else, with the same tax-free allowance. (If you invest any of your profits, the interest counts as your investment income and you will be taxed accordingly.) Your taxable profit is the amount of money you have been paid for your work or services or are due to be paid on invoices you have already issued, less allowable business expenses, capital allowances, stock relief.

Where your accounting year does not coincide with the tax year, it is the figures for the accounting year that you should supply.

Do not risk underdeclaring your income. Even if you are sure that you have no tax liability because your takings have been so small, you must include the source of income on the tax return.

You will be required to pay tax in two instalments on or before 1 January and the following 1 July respectively. If you do not pay by the specified time, and have not appealed within 30 days and applied to postpone payment of some or all of the tax, the

Inland Revenue may charge you interest on what you owe from those dates. There is an Inland Revenue form on which to make the appeal and apply for postponement. If your application for postponement is accepted, you are then only liable to pay the balance for which postponement has not been sought. If no application for postponement is submitted—whether the tax is excessive or not—you are legally obliged to pay the amount estimated by the inspector.

If your venture turns out to have been running at a loss, you can ask for the loss to be set against any other taxable income for the year in which you made the loss. Normally, however, the amount of the loss will be set against any profits in the following or subsequent years. From the 1978/79 tax year onwards, a loss made in any of the first four years of assessment of a new business which might reasonably be expected to make a profit, can be set against other income you had in the three tax years before the year in which you made the loss. This will bring you a tax repayment from Inland Revenue—but the calculations for such a tax rebate are complicated so you should ask the tax inspector for details, and consult an accountant.

loans

An advantage of having a bank account is that you may be allowed to operate with an overdraft should you have to pay out more than you get in for a while. But talk to the bank manager first. If you establish a good relationship with your bank manager and get him interested in your project, he may be a useful source of advice and information on your financial position and potential. You may be able to get a bank loan for a specific purchase or activity, such as an extension or adaptation of your premises.

You can claim as an allowable expense any interest you pay on a loan or overdraft for buying machinery or equipment for your work, provided the item qualified also as a capital allowance. The money must have been borrowed within a reasonable time of the purchase (generally, about three months).

When you approach someone for a loan, prepare a realistic report of your activities and plans, and the benefit you anticipate from the expenditure in question. Particularly when you are dealing with an intermediary, such as a bank manager, you will need to impress him with your abilities and potential because he is responsible to his superiors for lending you their money. You may be expected to provide reasonable security for the loan, such as your home or other property. Be careful to establish whether the rate of interest is fixed or variable, and check the effective annual rate of interest you will be paying, so that you do not find you are committed to higher repayments than you thought.

It is advisable to avoid spending more than is essential on capital expenditure when you start out on your venture. Excessive initial costs will tie up your money and you may find yourself working hard just to pay off a debt.

CHOICE OF WORK

This book does not deal with the professions or vocation in which people are self-employed and work from home, using part of their home as surgery, studio, consulting room, drawing office. Some people have no choice: the nature of their gift entails working independently—artists, composers, creative writers, for instance. Most of the other professionals decide at the outset of their career whether to practise privately or with others. Only someone with professional qualifications, experience and contacts can take up such work, or return to it, on a freelance basis. The relevant professional body can provide advice and information for members who are thinking of setting up on their own.

WITH PREVIOUS JOB EXPERIENCE

It may be possible to do at home work in which you have been trained and previously employed. Generally, it would not be worth learning the job from scratch in order to make use of it at home, and certainly not to do it at home without previous experience.

Beauty therapist, hairdresser

If you have been previously employed in any of the beauty professions—beautician, electrolysist, manicurist, hairdresser—you may well be able to set yourself up for clients to come to you at your home.

You will probably need to have planning permission from the local authority for this use of part of your house or flat. Some local authorities have bye-laws relating to hairdressing establishments and some may require registration.

You should set aside a room as a treatment room, and have a room in which clients can wait. Where possible, choose rooms which can be approached without having to go through the rest of the house. There should be access to a lavatory with a washbasin.

The treatment room must have enough space for the washbasin and equipment you use in the course of the treatment, and storage space for supplies of preparations you use.

You must be on the telephone. Keep an appointment book beside the instrument.

Initial outlay will be on equipment from specialist suppliers, and on furniture, including mirrors and suitable chairs, and on the installation of basins with a constant supply of hot water, and electric sockets. Ongoing costs include the electricity for lighting and heating water and rooms and for running driers and other apparatus. There will be laundry or washing costs for towels, wraps, linen. Supplies of hair preparations and cosmetics should be obtainable at wholesale prices.

Concentrate on local advertising, such as in newsagents' windows. A printed card with your name, address, telephone number and charges will help word of mouth recommendations. Your charges should reflect those asked locally in salons.

You must notify your insurers and be prepared to pay an additional premium for the extra risks, such as fire and damage to your equipment; cover for theft will be restricted. Insurance is desirable for your liability to clients arising from their being on your premises or from negligence in a treatment given by you. This will be difficult to obtain unless you are qualified (and even if you are, some risks are excluded). A special policy can be obtained from Lloyds through the Hairdressers Insurance Bureau (Apar House, 16 Selhurst Road, London SE25 5QF).

For brushing up your skill, there are special short courses at colleges, local or in London, and courses for the City and Guilds certificate in hairdressing. The British Association of Beauty Therapy and Cosmetology (secretary at 5 Greenways, Winchcombe, Cheltenham, Glos), and the National Health and Beauty Council (secretary at PO BOX 3, Studley, Warwicks) can give information about courses. The International Health and Beauty Council (PO BOX 36, Arundel, West Sussex BN18 0SW) issues diplomas and certificates of competence for students who have passed the examinations in, for example, facial treatment, remedial make-up, massage, manicure, pedicure. The IHBC also has information on home study courses.

Book-keeper

With experience in book-keeping, you can offer to help another freelancer or a small business with book-keeping problems, or do outwork for larger firms. The outlay is minimal—large desk or table, paper, pens, binders or files. Charge by the hour, and for expenses incurred for a particular job, such as telephone calls or fares, and for postage costs.

Advertise your services locally and in professional publications. You will need to keep your knowledge of tax requirements up-to-date.

Linguist

With a good knowledge of a foreign language, you can either teach or take conversation classes or set up as a translator.

Most translation work is technical. However good your command of the language, you also need specialist knowledge of a particular subject—about computers, or music, say. The most technical translations are the most highly paid (and the most difficult), the more obscure languages (such as arabic and japanese) command the highest rates.

It is advisable to translate into your mother tongue rather than into the foreign language. Stick to subjects you know, and do not take on things you are unfamiliar with 'just to oblige'—you are more likely to lose a disillusioned client than to oblige him.

There are a number of translation agencies who are useful for a start, but pay you less than they charge the client.

If you approach a publisher cold in the hope of getting literary translations, submit a sample of your work. For commercial or technical translations, advertise locally or put your name and details down in the reference department of the local library; prepare a short description of what you have to offer, have it photocopied or even printed and distribute it to local factories and offices, particularly those with an overseas market.

Charge per thousand words, or on a time basis if the work is fragmented (lists, indexes, catalogues).

The Translators Association (a group within the Society of Authors, 84 Drayton Gardens, London SW10 9SD) offers its members legal and general advice and assistance on matters relating to their work (but not the getting of it) and fees, including the vetting of contracts.

The Institute of Linguists (24a Highbury Grove, London N5 2EA) also can advise on rates and methods of charging, and give information; jobs are advertised in its journal. The Translators' Guild is the professional body for general and technical translators within the Institute of Linguists.

teaching
You can offer to give conversation classes in small groups. Charge for a series of classes—say, six to eight weeks in advance. Make clear the approximate standard of knowledge you expect of the group members (beginners, intermediate, advanced); possibly run separate classes for the different standards.

One-to-one tutoring can be either for conversation or preparing pupils for exams or for going abroad. Get in touch with a firm or business with overseas connections and offer to coach individuals being sent to the foreign country. You may be paid by the sponsoring body, on a retainer basis. Such teaching may entail evening lessons to fit in with a pupil's working hours.

Music teacher

With the requisite grades, you can teach your instrument at home, coaching children or students for Royal Schools of Music or similar external examinations. If you are a good player even without examination qualifications you can teach young children the basics, or give lessons to someone who just wants to play better without aiming for a series of exams. A more unusual instrument has a rarity value—but potential pupils may be rare, too.

You may have to take pupils in the evenings, to suit them. Use a separate room where misplaced notes will not bring complaints from family or neighbours. There is no capital outlay—pupils will provide their own instrument (except for the piano which, if a pianist, you presumably already have). Sheet music and books of music are expensive; let the pupils provide their own or pay for them.

Inform your insurance company, in case your policy needs to be extended to cover any extra risks or liability.

Young children will have to be brought to, and fetched from, lessons; if a pupil is accompanied by an adult, where possible try to encourage the adult to sit in another room because it is easier both for teacher and pupil to be uninhibited by a third party. Escorts will appreciate being able to wait comfortably the while, so some sort of (heated) waiting room or hall is essential.

Private teachers can join the Incorporated Society of Musicians (10 Stratford Place, London W1N 9AE) if they have a professional music qualification (or, exceptionally, they can qualify by reputation). The Society makes regular recommendations of minimum fees to be charged for private tuition and makes available to its members booklets of advice, standard forms of agreement and fees leaflets. Members of the private teachers section are listed in the Society's professional register of private teachers, a publication which is revised annually and sent to libraries, citizens advice bureaux and education authorities.

Teacher

To coach potential exam candidates in your subject, you need to know what the requirements are of the different examination levels, and the curricula. Even without formal teaching qualifications, someone with specialist knowledge can be a private tutor.

To find students, put a notice in the local paper, on newsagents' boards, at schools and colleges, churches, library, music and dramatic societies, and places where parents of young children or teenagers are likely to gather. You might even try the swimming pool, skating rink, sports clubs, leisure centre.

In some areas, there may be a demand for english to be taught to foreigners. You may be able to get such work through foreign embassies or consulates.

Charge per hour or series of lessons, and according to the standard of teaching required or level of exam. Relative strangers coming constantly to your premises may affect your insurance cover, particularly for theft.

by correspondence

You may prefer tutoring at a distance rather than face to face. The Association of British Correspondence Colleges (6 Francis Grove, London SW19 4DT) will send a list of member colleges, with subjects taught, and a list of accredited colleges is obtainable from the Council for the Accreditation of Correspondence Colleges (27 Marylebone Road, London NW1 5JS). Write to the colleges doing courses in your subject and offer your services. There are not many vacancies for tutors except in the less usual subjects.

When applying, list your qualifications and experience and say why you think you will make a good tutor and how many hours you can give per week. If you are accepted, the college gives instruction on how to mark and grade the students' papers and the type of criticism to give. You are paid for the number of papers marked or students tutored at rates varying with the subject and standard. The college reimburses you for postage.

The Open University sometimes advertises for part-time tutorial and counselling staff, or you could write direct to the tutor's office, Walton Hall, Milton Keynes MK7 6AA.

Typist

If you can type fast and accurately, buy (or hire) a good quality machine, preferably electric, with plenty of symbols. For 'golf-ball' machines, you can buy additional different type faces.

To get work, advertise your services widely—on student notice boards at the university (for theses) or colleges; by a handout to local businesses and societies, radio station, consultants, barristers' chambers; by advertisements in literary publications. State exactly what you offer and how much you charge.

Prepare samples of your work (letters, notices, plays, reports) to show prospective customers. If you have a play-back machine you can offer to accept transcribing work from tapes—but you have to be sure that the dictator's cassettes fit your machine.

Try to get your name on the record at publishers and literary agents; long jobs such as typing a book are a good standby. To advertise in *The Author* (84 Drayton Gardens, London SW10 9SD), you have first to provide two references and a sample of your work.

Charge per thousand words or per sheet of paper or by the hour. Manuscripts, much corrected work and tabulated work will take longer, so scale your charges accordingly. Charge for the paper and any carbon paper used. Paper is heavy so try not to have to use the post for delivering your finished work.

Use a room apart from the rest of the household, if possible, and where neighbours will not be disturbed by your tapping at all hours.

You will have to be prepared to type for many hours on end, about subjects that do not interest you. Take on only what you are sure you can complete; other people's typing may be uninteresting to you, but to them it is vital to have it back in the time set and perfectly typed. Much of the work will be rush jobs, left by the author/producer to the last moment, so be careful not to take on more than you can manage within the deadline set.

Once you have accepted work, complete it—if necessary, staying up until three in the morning—and learn the lesson not to take on too much the next time.

through an agency
If you hope to get work through a typing agency, do not offer to do work at home without having a decent typewriter; be prepared to take a sample of work done on it when you register. When you do work for an agency, check whether you will count as an employee for tax and national insurance purposes.

Do not ring up for work except when you are free of other commitments and thoroughly organised for it. If you are offered work and refuse it more than once or twice, even if your work is very good you are unlikely to be offered any again. Agencies do not like wasting time on trying people who keep saying 'no'.

If you have a genuine reason—such as a child getting ill, a death in the family—for being unable to complete the task, be willing to deliver the rest of the job to someone else whom the agency may find to take over from you.

To start a typing agency yourself from home, you need to apply and pay for a licence from the regional office of the Department of Employment. (The licence fee is £108 a year.) It is against the law to operate as an agency without the licence, and against the law for an agency to advertise without making it clear that it is an agency.

duplicating

A related service you could offer would be duplicating and photocopying. A new machine costs a lot of money; with a secondhand machine, you risk more frequent breakdowns. So it may be a better proposition to lease the machine you want (around £50 a month) and to have a contract for service and maintenance. You can then change the model to something more sophisticated, if you find it inadequate for your use. As well as the basic rental, you may be charged per number of copies run off.

You may want to invest in a machine for collating or folding printed material.

You will need to be able to buy and store suitable paper in large enough quantities to get a discount from the supplier. Many of the items used with these machines are highly flammable, so you will need to have safe storage space—and adjust your insurance for the extra risk.

The machines take up quite a lot of space and have to be positioned where they can be plugged into electric sockets (make use of the cheaper night-rate tariff, where you can). Some machines, especially for duplicating, are fairly noisy when operating, so you may have to shut them away to avoid irritating the rest of the household or neighbours.

It is usual to charge per sheet of paper copied or duplicated; the overheads should include depreciation on a machine you have bought, and electricity consumed.

DOING WORK AT HOME FOR AN EMPLOYER

Many of the people who work at home for an outside employer are doing the type of work generally done in a factory—assembling anything from watch straps to fire extinguishers, making toys or lampshades, filling Christmas crackers, finishing textile products. A lot of such work is done for the clothing industry. Much of the work is repetitive, requires little skill (but attention) and does not lead to the satisfaction of seeing the finished product. Women who had reached a highly skilled grade in factory work are sometimes asked to do work at home of a more specialised nature than the normal type of homework, and get much better rates of pay.

Other types of outwork, such as typing, addressing envelopes, data preparation, invisible mending, are done on an agency basis for a freelance agent or for a firm or shop.

There are no employment agencies specifically for outwork, so if you are thinking of doing this kind of work, the best places to look are the job columns in your local newspaper, notices in jobcentres, advertisements in magazines and on newsagents' boards. Ignore advertisements requesting payment for sending directories of homework or lists of employers: most are useless and some have been found fraudulent.

Some employers request a 'token of goodwill' before sending the first homework job. These, too, are better avoided. Do not send any money. Some sharp operators, realising that there is an overwhelming demand for homework, have cashed in on other people's need, and neither work nor 'employer' materialises.

If you do find acceptable homework, try to negotiate about the volume and regularity of work, and find out before committing yourself what the work involves in the way of equipment and materials. You may be expected to store bulky containers of stuffing for toys or plastic foam for packaging, to use flammable and/or nasty-smelling adhesives or paints, to leave awkward articles around the room to dry, to work with irritant substances or a noisy machine. Knives and other sharp instruments or poisonous substances will be a hazard if there are young children in the household.

Homeworkers are, in theory, given the protection of the Health and Safety at Work Act in that the suppliers of homework have a duty to ensure as far as is reasonably practicable that you are not exposed to risks. The major responsibility for ensuring dangerous substances are not used in homework therefore lies with the supplier. There is also some obligation on workers to ensure that, in carrying out the work, they do not put themselves or other members of their household at risk. As yet, however, there are no adequate administrative arrangements for enforcing the provisions of the act. Nevertheless, homeworkers, like any other workers, are entitled to get in touch with the local health and safety executive office and make a complaint about any danger to health arising from their working conditions.

You could run into difficulties with the environmental health department of the local authority if there is a complaint that you create a 'nuisance', for instance by the use of an industrial sewing machine or other noisy equipment. Not surprisingly, neighbours may be less tolerant of noise or fumes than the homeworker. It has often been via a complaint of this sort that a homeworker has discovered rules he or she was unaware of in a tenancy agreement which restricts the right to work at home, or that planning permission is required for changing the use of the premises.

employment protection
Homeworkers as such are not included in the legislation incorporated in the Employment Protection (Consolidation) Act which gives entitlement to redundancy payment, maternity pay or compensation for unfair dismissal. In order to prove their claim to any of these payments they have to establish employee status before a tribunal. Facts taken into account by the tribunal would be, for example, that all work was delivered and collected daily (or even perhaps weekly) by one firm or supplier or that the firm has been deducting tax and national insurance from the worker's pay. The number of hours worked is important, too: a part-time worker who has been working less than 16 hours a week is not qualified to get redundancy payment or to claim unfair dismissal.

A Homeworkers' Association has been formed, whose aim is to extend existing legislation to cover homeworkers; that work done at home should be paid on an equal rate to that completed in the factory, with a premium to cover homeworkers' overhead costs; and that employers should be required to provide details of homework done for them to the Department of Employment. The address of the Homeworkers' Association is c/o The Low Pay Unit, 9 Poland Street, London W1V 3DG (telephone 01-437 1780). The Association issues a newsletter, free to homeworkers.

pay
In most cases, the pay for outwork is decided by direct individual negotiation with the supplier. Rates of pay vary widely and there are no hard and fast rules. It is worth remembering that there are hidden costs to homework besides the inconvenience of using the home as a surrogate factory and warehouse. Industrial sewing machines or other equipment needed

may be expensive to run (and if not supplied, cost a lot to buy) and employers often take it for granted that homeworkers will supply smaller items like needles and thread. It is vital to take these extra costs into account in any negotiations.

Collection and delivery of work can be costly and inconvenient. Try to get the employing firm to do this for you, or at least to reimburse you.

Outwork is usually paid for on a piece work basis: a certain amount for each complete article or series of articles. The result is that many homeworkers are unaware of what they are paid for an hour's work. To avoid slaving for next to nothing, do a simple check: give the job your complete attention for an hour (allowing a little for the improvement you may make with practice) and see how much or how many you have achieved in that time. Then calculate your hourly rate of pay by multiplying the amount paid to you per unit of work completed by the number you can make in an hour. For example, if you are paid £1 for every 10 items (i.e. 10p each) and can complete six in an hour, the hourly rate is 60p. But this does not take account of overheads.

A fast worker will obviously earn more than a slow worker; an average worker should be able to earn at least the minimum rate, where this is set by statute.

wages councils
Homeworkers in the some trades have minimum rates of pay
laid down for them by the appropriate wages council. In 1979,
the minimum rates set by wages councils ranged from about
80p an hour to just over £1.10 an hour.

Wages councils were established for specific trades under the
Wages Councils Act 1959. They include

Boot and Shoe Repairing
Button Manufacturing
Corset
Dressmaking and Women's
   Light Clothing
Hat, Cap and Millinery
Lace Finishing
Linen and Cotton Handkerchief
   and Household Goods
Made-up Textiles
Ostrich and Fancy Feather and
   Artificial Flower

Perambulator and Invalid
   Carriage
Pin, Hook and Eye and Snap
   Fastener
Ready-made and Wholesale
   Bespoke Tailoring
Retail Bespoke Tailoring
Rope, Twine and Net
Sack and Bag
Shirtmaking
Toy Manufacturing
Wholesale Mantle and Costume

The main function of a wages council is to fix the statutory
minimum remuneration to be paid by employers, either generally or for any particular work, and other terms and conditions
of employment, such as holiday pay. Rates fixed by an employer
in a trade covered by a wages council must be adequate to
cover any necessary expenditure incurred by the worker in
connection with the employment. If they are not, the employer
must refund the expenditure.

These terms and conditions must be observed by all employers
of the workers concerned and are enforceable at law. A leaflet

explaining the Wages Councils Act briefly and listing all the wages councils is available from the Department of Employment, 8 St James Square, London SW1Y 4JB, and from citizens advice bureaux.

There are wages inspectors throughout the country to enforce the minimum rates of pay; they can make an employer pay up in full and also pay any arrears that have built up from work already done. Complaints are investigated confidentially, but should your employer guess the origin of the complaint and take unwarranted action (such as withdrawing all work), get in touch with the Homeworkers' Association who may be able to do something.

For homeworkers outside the scope of wages councils, little can be done about underpayment unless they are working on a government contract or are members of a trades union (few homeworkers are). Someone who is working on a government contract being paid less than the wages established for the industry in the area where the work is being carried out can make a claim under the Fair Wages Resolution. (You do not have to be a member of a trades union to do so.) A claim under this resolution ends up at the central arbitration committee but should, initially, be made to the Department of Employment. If possible, the claim should include details of the contract. A leaflet on the Fair Wages Resolution is available from the Department of Employment.

USING AN EXISTING SKILL

Previous knowledge and experience by way of a hobby can be turned into a money-making activity. The gifted amateur can exploit his existing aptitude by working at home, using his skill and interest in an organised way for profit.

It is important not only to establish but to maintain a high standard for your work: the 80th teddybear must be just as well made and attractive as the first; your 50th quiche as firmly set and flavoured as the two you made for your first party.

GETTING BETTER AT IT

Before commercialising your hobby, interest or skill, you should ensure that it is of a high enough standard. For instance, handmade objects need particularly high standards of design, style, quality and execution: people who buy handmade objects do so because they are basically discriminating and generally looking for things that are beautifully conceived and carefully made.

For most skills, particularly handicrafts, there are a number of books giving practical hints and advice on how to make/produce/maintain/mend/restore whatever it is you are concerned with. Go to your local library and ask for a bibliography or look in the index or on the shelves for your particular subject and borrow copies of the most relevant titles. The do-it-yourself and handyman magazines are an unending source of hints and explanations on practical activities, and there are magazines and journals covering most technical and professional occupations which it could be worth subscribing to, even if only for a few months before you get established. These may also provide you with possible sales outlets, through advertisements or articles. Consult *Willing's Press Guide* in the library to find out what is being published in your line and by whom.

Ask at your local library about any courses in the area. Many colleges of further education and polytechnics run courses for people who are thinking about going back to work or starting a new career. The courses are short (usually one day a week for ten weeks) and you need no qualifications to apply.

You may find that your local education authority or Workers' Educational Association is running a course which could help you to earn money in some way, even if that is not the primary purpose of the course. Adult education courses run by a local authority may be in the daytime or evening. The charges are low (for residents of the area) and there is generally a very wide range of subjects. Motives for taking courses vary, so try to make sure that you join a class where the others are likely to be serious students who want to learn more about the subject and are not there just for the entertainment.

Courses, full and part-time, are run in colleges of further education and similar colleges for the City and Guilds of London Institute's certificates in a wide range of technical and some craft subjects. Information about the courses and examinations leading to City and Guilds certificates can be obtained from the Institute, 76 Portland Place, London WIN 4AA.

An annual guide to full-time and sandwich courses at polytechnics in England and Wales is available from the Committee of Directors of Polytechnics, 309 Regent Street, London WIR 7PE; price around £4 but available at reference libraries.

The Department of Education and Science Regional Advisory Council publishes each year a compendium (£1.60) of advanced courses including some unusual ones in colleges of further and higher education outside the universities.

Many people who cannot go out to study could work on a course at home. It is possible to study many subjects through a correspondence college. The Association of British Correspondence Colleges (6 Francis Grove, London SW19 4DT) will send a list of its member colleges and the subjects they cover. A list of correspondence colleges accredited by the Council for the Accreditation of Correspondence Colleges (an independent charity officially recognised by the Department of Education and Science) is available from the Council (27 Marylebone Road, London NW1 5JS). Both these bodies offer a free information and advisory service on any aspects of correspondence education.

A *Which?* report on correspondence courses in August 1977 discussed how to choose a course and college, suggesting points to watch out for, and gave the results of a survey of members who had taken courses.

You could use one of the BBC's series of further education programmes or one of the ITV series on, say, toymaking or patchwork to improve your own technique to a more professional standard. For information about the BBC's courses, write to Educational Broadcasting Information (30/CE), BBC, London W1A 1AA; for ITV, to your local programme company or the education officer of the Independent Broadcasting Authority (70 Brompton Road, London SW3 1EY). BBC local radio stations each have an education producer, and broadcast a range of programmes appropriate to the needs of people in that area.

Short residential courses are run for their members by the National Federation of Women's Institutes at Denman College, Marcham, Abingdon, Oxon OX13 6NW. These include courses called 'Back to work', 'Market gardening' 'The tourist in your home'. There are always more applications than places. The National Institute of Adult Education publishes a calendar of residential short courses (50p from NIAE, 19B de Montfort Street, Leicester LE1 7GH).

If you are able to manage a short full-time course, it may be worth asking your local education authority for details of their discretionary grant awards scheme (if any) and an application form.

Cooking

Unless you are already quite experienced at cooking, baking, sweet making, for family or friends, you should not consider making money out of doing so for other people. The three main categories of cookery for other people are making things (cakes, pies, jams, sweets, bread) for sale; providing meals, teas, coffee, snacks, for people to eat in your home; preparing dishes at home for other people's parties, dinners, lunches, receptions.

If you want to develop or perfect your skill, you could do an advanced cookery course at a local adult institute or take a course at a technical college for a City and Guilds catering examination. The National Federation of Women's Institutes basic certificates in home economics include bakery and food preservation (herbs, jams, pickles). The examination for this certificate can be taken by non-WI members who attend a local education authority course. If a WI member, you may be able to go on one of the Women's Institute week or weekend residential courses at Denman College in Oxfordshire. More advanced courses costing several hundred pounds can be taken at the Cordon Bleu school or Leith's school in London; there are year-long waiting lists for some courses.

There are statutory requirements under the Food Hygiene (General) Regulations 1970 (SI 1172; from HMSO, 12½p) about the preparation and sale of food to be consumed by the public. The principal requirements relate to the cleanliness of the premises and equipment used, the hygienic handling of food, the temperatures at which certain foods are to be kept, the provision of water supply and washing facilities, the disposal of waste materials, and the construction and maintenance of the premises used for the purposes of a food business.

If you let the environmental health department of your local authority know that you are intending to sell food to the public, before the scheme has gone past the initial idea stage, an environmental health officer will come to inspect your kitchen premises and equipment and storage facilities, and can make the necessary recommendations about complying with the appropriate legislation. He will be concerned about pets being allowed into the kitchen and about other domestic uses of a normal kitchen, such as washing of clothes.

You should also consult your local planning authority in case you need planning permission for a change of use.

In Northern Ireland, anyone who provides food to be consumed on the premises by the general public has to meet the requirements of the Development of Tourist Traffic Act and be registered with the Northern Ireland Tourist Board and visited by the Board's inspectorate staff.

With any form of catering, there are food poisoning risks, particularly if handling delicate ingredients such as shellfish and the re-heating of precooked food. So notify your insurers and ask about public liability cover.

For cooking in quantities, you will probably need quite a lot of additional utensils, large dishes and extra gadgets; also aluminium foil or plastic film for covering and wrapping prepared dishes, and plenty of cool storage space. A freezer will help, but a big refrigerator may be even more useful. You may find later that you need an extra oven or a second cooker. Your fuel consumption will be high, so remember to cost this in to the prices you charge. Also allow for the increased rates you may have to pay.

Try to find a source for buying ingredients in bulk, such as flour, sugar, dried fruit, and make use of catering packs of fats and jams, tea, coffee and cooking oil, and similar supplies. Although you can save money by buying in this way, it may not be economic if you have to travel a fair distance to get to the appropriate cash-and-carry store or warehouse. You will need a large car or a van to transport the bulk packs you buy, and adequate storage space at home. Foodstuff is only worth buying in this way if you will be using it relatively quickly (before the bottom of a 10 kilo pack has gone stale or bad), and you must have somewhere to keep the containers of food dry and clean and at the right temperature for the contents. *The Grocer* magazine publishes an annual marketing directory listing cash-and-carries geographically throughout the country and giving a list of food trade organisations. It costs £4; ask for it in your library. Information about wholesale fruit markets is given in the annual handbook (£3.50) of the National Federation of Fruit and Potato Trades, which also lists their members and other relevant organisations.

for sale
Making cakes or confectionery or biscuits for selling through a local shop or cafe has the advantage that you can probably time the work to your own convenience—although, if successful, you may have to work hard to keep up with demand.

It would be a good idea to specialise in a particular line which other people are unlikely to make: unusual chutneys or pickles, lardy cakes, sweets or toffees or fudge, profiteroles or eclairs for filling, and seasonal fare such as simnel cake at Easter, yule log at Christmas, wedding cakes or birthday cakes. Home-made bread and rolls are always popular, even though more people nowadays make their own. So is other yeast baking—doughnuts, crumpets, croissants, danish pastries—which many women do not have time to do themselves. But for most of these things, assess carefully how much time you have to put into it for fairly small returns: it is difficult to charge enough and make enough without pricing yourself out of the market.

Jams, jellies, chutneys, pickles, marmalade, mincemeat, are all likely to be good sellers, but some take a lot of preparing and processing. You need to have a reliable source of cheap fruit, either what you grow yourself or what you can pick at a nearby market garden or from friends' unwanted crops. Preserving sugar will be a major outlay, and you will need a supply of glass jars and tops. Labels should be attractive, and clearly marked with your name and address and the content of the jar (weight as well as description and date).

You may be able to rent a stall at a local market. Someone living in the country could become a shareholder in the WI market society (5p for life). You can then sell your goodies on the weekly market stall, charging the cost of making them plus 33 per cent; the WI gets a commission on the takings. Ask locally about a market in your area, or write to the National Federation of WIs (39 Eccleston Street, London SW1W 9NT; enclose a stamped addressed envelope) to find out where there are market societies. There are quite stringent requirements about the presentation and labelling of products to make sure that the statutory and the WI regulations are met. Nothing, whether cooked or uncooked, that has been in a freezer may be sold at a WI market.

Whenever and whatever you are selling, it helps to display your produce attractively—in a basket or bowl, wrapped or in a labelled jar. Where possible, show your name and address (for repeat orders).

Ask whether a nearby stately home or castle or museum or gallery, hotels and post offices and tourist board will put up a notice about the home-made food you have to offer.

meals at home
If you are going to serve teas or refreshments or other meals in your home or garden, it is profitable to have a speciality such as 'olde englishe' teas, or traditional dishes. As well as advertising locally, you could try the newsletter or journal of organisations such as the British Tourist Authority and any guide books or leaflets about the area.

The initial outlay for serving food in your house or garden will be for chairs, tables, crockery, tableware and table mats and cloths, napkins. Towels and soap for washbasins and lavatory paper are other items that will need constant replenishing and which you should try to buy in wholesale quantities.

You may have to install extra lavatories and washbasins, for which you will probably need planning permission; also for providing car parking facilities, for which you may, in addition, need the consent of the highway authority.

You must, by law, display the prices you charge for all items, from set teas to individual biscuits, and describe your products and ingredients accurately. When your turnover takes you over the VAT threshold, you will have to become registered and add the required percentage to the price of items consumed on the premises (VAT does not apply to most taken-away food). If you decide at any time to sell cigarettes, you will count as an 'excise trader' so that a customs officer has the right to come and inspect your premises (looking, for instance, for smuggled tobacco) at any time.

catering
If you are catering for business lunches, you can cook all the food at home and take it to an office. You will need some suitable form of transport and, if you have to provide cutlery and plates, you need to be able to afford the original outlay—unless you can persuade the business firms that it is a good idea to have their own utensils. Advertisements in the local paper may produce customers.

When catering for special events—weddings, parties, lunches, dinners—you must plan properly and be disciplined about preparing in good time, as for a military exercise. It is a good idea to help out at big private or charity functions to see how things are organised and to get experience before you take on big parties yourself. You may need to get a like-minded friend (or two) to help with some occasions, for a fee or a share in the takings.

Consider early on if you want to stock up with a set of china, glass and cutlery; having them to offer for hire with your catering services may help you get the job. Outside hire firms can be expensive to resort to, or may not exist in your locality.

Be prepared to offer alternative menus at different prices, and to do a breakdown and quote your charges at so-much per head. Remember to cost in your own time properly. It is a temptation, when you like cooking, to do it for love and to forget that your time should be profitably as well as agreeably used.

Drawing and illustrating

You can make use of a talent for drawing or painting without being a full-time professional artist. But you must realise that you will be competing with a professional's high standard of work, creatively and technically.

There are evening and residential courses on drawing and painting, including portraits, in many colleges and institutes, and summer courses on sketching—which could be useful to improve or expand your natural aptitude.

If you can make drawings or paintings of people's children, pets, houses or gardens, you can try to get commissions either by word of mouth recommendations or by advertising locally. But do not spoil your chances by taking on a commission to paint someone's child when you are really only good at flowers or houses: better to refuse a commission than to gain a reputation for unsatisfactory work.

Canvas, frames, oil-paint are major expenses; so are good paper or board, and you may need a variety of colours and qualities. You may be able to arrange special terms with a local stationer or art supply shop.

To sell work that has not been done on commission, you have to be able to show it. When you have enough of it to make a good display, craft shops can be a good place to show your work. Although you may not want to be considered an amateur, joining a local amateur society may give you a chance to exhibit—and sell.

Pen-and-ink drawings of local scenes can be printed on a good quality photocopier and made into notelets, calendars, Christmas cards and prints for framing. It would add to the price and interest of the printed pen-and-ink drawings if they were coloured by hand.

Cards can be sold through local shops or at charity fairs and bazaars (but you will have to hand over a proportion of your takings to the good cause). You could try sending examples of your work to a few charities, in case any would be prepared to commission you to design cards or notelets or calendars or other decorative wares for their mail order lines. And the large manufacturers of greetings cards might be interested in a new design. This would entail a contract covering copyright, royalties and other conditions.

If you know someone who writes suitable children's stories, or can write them yourself, you could illustrate these. A joint production of this kind, if good enough, might find a publisher more readily than the story on its own.

Dressmaking

In order to make money from dressmaking, you must have a high professional standard. Many people want their clothes to have the individual fit, style and finishing that only a personal dressmaker can provide. But they will expect a higher standard than from ready-to-wear clothes. Other people who will need you are the tall, the plump, and the unusual-shaped.

Courses on dressmaking and tailoring are available throughout the country at most centres of further education. A course for the City and Guilds certificate in tailoring could be useful. There are private schools who specialise in these subjects. For instance, the School of Dressmaking and Design at 69 Wells Street, London W1P 3RB runs an intensive four-month course covering dressmaking, patternmaking, fashion designing, grading. The Sew-In School at the same address offers less expensive fun-to-sew courses.

Television programmes are helpful from time to time, and there will be many books on the subject in your library. Specialist suppliers for the fashion clothing trade include R D Franks Ltd (Market Place, London WIN 8EJ) whose catalogue covers books on dressmaking, pattern cutting, patchwork, embroidery, tailoring, and workroom equipment.

Your sewing machine should have standard attachments for zips and gathering. A swing-needle action for buttonholes and overedging is helpful, and so is a reverse stitch for the ends of

seams. Equipment for pressing should include a steam iron, sleeve board and dressmaker's ham.

Ideally, you should set aside one room for sewing only, with good lighting for your machine, a large cutting table, ironing board permanently up, dressmaker's dummy, hanging space for clothes and patterns, storage space for fabrics and trimmings. Keep leftover pieces of material graded by fabric and colour to make up packs of scraps to sell to patchwork enthusiasts.

Your room for fittings should be private, and warm, and have a good mirror. Keep an appointments book.

Cost your work at an hourly rate, and charge for all time devoted to the customer's needs—shopping, making, fitting. When estimating how much to charge, be clear whether it is you or the customer who supplies the fabric, lining, buttons, zips, and who does the shopping for them. If customers want to provide their own fabric and patterns, try to make sure that they supply a pattern which bears a fairly close resemblance to the finished article they want: otherwise, you can find yourself doing time-consuming and perhaps not totally satisfactory pattern alterations, and even complete re-designs. It can be helpful to keep a supply of pattern books handy, so that customers can show you what they want and you can make sure that they know what is involved in terms of quantity and types of material.

It helps both you and the customer to be able to give an estimate of time and cost at the outset. If a customer wants a rush job, do not accept it unless you can adjust your other work.

You may need to spend money on occasional advertisements, to supplement word-of-mouth recommendations.

alterations and repairs

Shops and stores selling off-the-peg clothing to both sexes usually undertake alterations for their customers and make a charge for the service. The work includes shortening or lengthening sleeves, hemlines, and trouser legs; taking in or letting out waists, skirts, trousers, and jackets; improving or adding surface stitching. These alterations are often done off the premises by private dressmakers and tailors, so call on local shops and ask if you can do some for them. The sales assistant usually notes the alteration required and the shop may deliver and collect, or an arrangement could be made to visit the shop, say, twice a week.

Repairs are something different again: replacing zips, renewing pockets, replacing linings, changing buttons, strengthening broken seams, and invisibly mending holes. Dry cleaning shops are an outlet for this kind of work; shops may be willing to bring the work to you if you cannot collect it.

home machining

The clothing industry throughout the country uses many homeworkers with dressmaking and tailoring abilities. Generally speaking, a home machinist is required only to machine the garments; the pressing, buttonholes, buttons, and finishing are done by the manufacturer later.

Pay is generally by piece rates—that is, an agreed price per garment—with all the parts supplied cut and ready for machining together. Rates vary from manufacturer to manufacturer and with the quality and work content of each style. (Wages councils' minimum rates for dressmaking and tailoring average out at just over £1 an hour.) Standards in cheap garments are lower—no underpressing, fewer machine stitches per inch (or cm), no hand-sewing—and so are rates of pay.

The delivery is made in bundles; bundles of the same style and colour offer continuity, and the best opportunity for profit to the machinist. Switching of colours and styles entails thread changes, breaks in rhythm, and loss of time.

This kind of work could be found through an advertisement in the *Drapers Record, Fashion Weekly,* or local papers.

Knitting

Knitting by hand and knitting by machine are two entirely different skills.

Machine knitters are limited in what they can do. But what they can do, they can do so much more rapidly than the hand knitter that they can stay within the range of what people are willing to pay.

Knitting machines have much in common with sewing machines but some knitting machines are more complex than a domestic sewing machine, on the whole cost more, and for some people are more difficult to master.

Some local authorities run courses on machine knitting, and anyone buying a new machine should be sure to get a comprehensive demonstration from the manufacturer's representative. You may be able to get an almost new secondhand machine at a fraction of the original price.

You should, if possible, set aside a room for the machine and ironing board to be kept up, with plenty of storage space. Keep careful notes of customers' measurements and requirements (in case of repeat orders) and the time you spend (for costing).

Machine knitting, a Pan Craft book (£1.50) by Hazel Ratcliffe, includes advice on knitting for profit—for instance, that you, not the customer, should provide the wool or yarn.

The Worldwide Machine Knitters' Club (2 Town Bridge Buildings, Park Road, Pontypool, Gwent NP4 6YW) provides its members with advice on problems and queries about machine knitting, special offers from yarn manufacturers, free patterns, the quarterly journal, a chance to attend educational courses arranged by the club, contact with local knitting clubs.

hand-knitting

Knitting on pins or needles is more versatile than machine knitting, and is its basis. With the advent of knitting machines, much of the call for hand-knitting has vanished: it is uneconomic to hand-knit for sale anything that could be made equally well but much faster on a knitting machine.

Hand-knitting comes into its own with fabrics or patterns which are too complex or awkward for domestic machines. Aran is a good example of this but not Fair Isle which many machines can do very well.

Shops and spinners need hand-knitters for testing sets of instructions and for producing display garments, but the pay, reckoned by the hour, is very low. Rates are related to the thickness of the yarn and the complexity of the product. Write direct to the spinners whose yarn you like and ask if they require anyone. Each has a different entry test, and different requirements for making up the work—some prefer you to do it, others not. But whoever you produce for will want clean work done at the correct tension (most important), so you will have to work with care and accuracy. There is also a small market for baby garments.

The British Hand Knitting Association (Lloyds Bank Chambers, Hustlergate, Bradford, West Yorkshire BD1 1NU) can supply the names and addresses of yarn manufacturers who are its members.

Some hand-knitters find an outlet for their skills by doing freelance designing either for spinners or for placing in women's magazines or the women's pages of daily papers. Also, a few work in close collaboration with specialist spinners or colourists who need their vaguely-described ideas to be embodied in real stitches.

When hand-knitting or crocheting for a customer, it is difficult to charge a realistic price for the time spent: not many people would be willing to pay over £100 for a pullover. In order to bring the selling price to an acceptable figure, you may find that your notional pay per hour comes to under 30p.

Photography

A skilful and experienced amateur photographer could specialise in portrait photography (babies, children, adults, animals), especially in a place where there is no photographic studio in the neighbourhood. Or go out to record local events such as weddings, birthday parties, parades, fetes, dances and other social or sporting occasions.

There are courses in photography at adult education institutes and colleges, including residential ones; some are specifically for a type of photography—landscape, colour, portrait. There is a City and Guilds certificate course in photography.

Quite a lot of paper work is involved, and an efficient filing and recording system is necessary. Set up a room to use as a dark room with all the necessary developing and printing equipment if you decide to do your own processing. Generally, black-and-white work can be undertaken in domestic surroundings with advantage in speed and cost, and possibly a better product. Colour is more difficult and demands a higher capital investment, so it is probably better to let a professional laboratory do it for you. A small local firm can generally produce the work more cheaply than you can do it for yourself.

For portrait photography, to get technically good results you will need a suitable room to use as a studio, and good lighting and equipment. Backgrounds are important: two or three rolls of different shades and colours of paper are useful. Provide a mirror in the reception area or waiting room.

You may need two or three cameras, to suit different types of subject, and a spare while one is being serviced or mended. Since lenses seldom go wrong, with interchangeable types it suffices to have one set of lenses and two bodies. Do not assume that you have to have the most expensive equipment—skilled use of a simple camera can be just as effective as the most elaborate apparatus (even if less impressive to the client). Subscribing to a photographer's journal (a subscription can be set against tax, as a business expense) will provide you with up-to-date information about latest technical developments; go to professional photographic exhibitions to get ideas.

Get your supplies of paper and films and other materials direct from the suppliers, on wholesale terms. If you link yourself to one of the big photographic firms, you may get a special discount in return for advertising their wares by your use of them.

A local art shop or gallery may be willing to display a notice about your services; estate agents or auctioneers may want photographs taken of what they are selling.

Put an advertisement in the local paper, and have printed cards to distribute. Make use of the announcement columns in the papers for new babies, future weddings, forthcoming anniversaries or special events. For weddings, make contact with the local vicar, ministers and register office; remember brides can come back for baby pictures.

It can be profitable to offer the finished photograph(s) in a special album or frame provided (and charged for) by you. Usually, charges are made on the basis of, say, 'Three $5 \times 7\frac{1}{2}$ inch prints in folders and one 10×8 inch in special frame for £xx. Extra enlargements available according to list.'

If someone commissions you to take a photograph, the copyright belongs to him. Although it is customary for you to retain the negative, you cannot use the photograph (say, for display) without his permission. And if you charge too much for extra prints, he may just get the original one copied.

An alternative line to supplement commissioned orders would be to offer your photographs of suitable subjects or objects to publishers (newspaper or magazine), greetings card manufacturers or illustrated magazines for reproduction. Blockmakers work from black-and-white glossy prints or colour transparencies; they do not like reproducing from ordinary colour prints. Slides should not be mounted in glass: use plastic sleeves.

In general, photographs are sold to magazines on the basis of one reproduction right. However, although the copyright (and negative) remains the property of the photographer, it would be unethical, and in the long run inadvisable, to submit the same picture to another magazine in the same field, at least until several years had passed. If in doubt, tell the editor and let him decide.

The *Writers' and Artists' Yearbook* lists photographic agents specialising in different fields, such as botany, art, child studies, for specialist or technical publications, calendars. But read the small print concerning agents' commission.

When sending out your work, label each print clearly, identifying it as yours with your name, address and telephone number (and make a note of what you have shown to whom). Type captions and fix them to the back of the print—do not write on the back of prints as the ink offsets onto the next print. If there is the slightest possibility of a picture being reproduced the wrong way up, mark clearly which is the top. Flower close-ups are particularly liable to be inverted. Send return postage to make sure of getting your work back.

Flat fees are more common than royalties for photographs. You may be asked to relinquish the copyright if the photographs are to be published in a book. If so, your fee should be higher. The important point is to know what you are selling and not to relinquish more rights than essential to ensure a sale.

With illustrated articles, most magazines pay by the page as published. An editor will always tell you in advance what he will pay and you can then decide if it is worth your while.

If you need legal advice and help with a contract or copyright problem, you could get in touch with Artlaw Services (358 Strand, London WC2R OHS; telephone 01-240 0610), a non-profit-making organisation established to give free information, advice and help to visual artists and craftsmen on legal problems in relation to their work. There is a voluntary subscription scheme (£5 a year).

Articles for magazines can be accompanied by photographs. If you do not write articles yourself, you may wish to cooperate with an author and provide photographic illustrations. Keep on friendly terms with picture editors. They are often asked to suggest photographers for specialised subjects and can steer work your way.

Printing

Most local bye-laws classify printing as light industry, so when part-time printing moves out of the hand-press phase and the profitable hobby becomes more of a small business, trouble can be expected if you do not have planning permission. Also, inform your insurance company and increase your cover to include machinery and paper.

The covenants on many houses carry restrictions on operating a business, particularly where machinery of any nature is involved. The noise and neighbours should be allowed for.

There are City and Guilds examinations in printing techniques but facilities for learning the craft of printing are not widespread. Most of the print training courses are run as part of day courses for printing apprentices, and places for outsiders are limited.

Books (from the public library) are a good first source of information, and so are instruction leaflets and manuals issued by Adana Ltd (15–19 Church Street, Twickenham, Middlesex TW1 3NN), who are the only remaining manufacturers in England of small hand-operated printing machines.

Printing demands a fair amount of capital investment even if you buy a secondhand machine. You should be able to buy paper and card from a wholesaler. Value added tax is chargeable on paper; but printed booklets, brochures, pamphlets and leaflets are zero-rated. Customs and Excise leaflet 6/76/VLC deals with the VAT liability of printed matter.

Advertise yourself by word of mouth and in local publications and by putting (carefully printed) cards in newsagents' windows or other relevant vantage points. Ask the local chamber of commerce, schools, a college or university, local cultural, educational and commercial societies and groups, even the local council, whether you can print newsletters, invitations or notices of events for them. Initially, it may be simpler to concentrate on invitation cards, letterheads, small posters. For other work, you may need the use of other machines, such as a collator and binder for books, folder for brochures and pamphlets, guillotine.

The British Printing Society (secretary at 14 Penrose Avenue West, Liverpool L14 6UT), whose members are full-time and part-time printers, has regular monthly publications, a large postal lending library and also local branches in most areas. There is a commercial section for those who print for profit, which issues a number of publications to help the small jobbing printer, including marketing information and a variety of technical advice. The extra fee for membership of the commercial group includes a practical printers handbook, costing system and other commercial aids. Full details can be obtained from Comprint Services, 44 Boldmere Road, Sutton Coldfield, West Midlands; send a large stamped addressed envelope for specimen publications.

Repair work

You will in many cases have to invest not only in the cost of the materials used but spend a lot of your time and thought and skill in putting an article back into a near-perfect state. Your charge for each job must reflect this outlay as well as the visible (or invisible) restoration.

Even if you are not specifically asked, give an estimate of what you are going to charge when you accept an article for repair or restoration. This gives the customer the chance to withdraw rather than make difficulties after you have invested your time and money in the work.

You may be housing some quite valuable objects, and will need to keep them safe. You can insure for their loss or damage by fire while at your premises, or theft where there has been forcible entry, but not for unexplained loss or for damage you do while working on them. Even where you can get insurance, the problem of value arises: you only have the owner's word for it and, even quite innocently, many people are under the impression that their picture, clock, book, is worth a lot more than it really is. Theoretically, you should ask each customer for proof of value and authentication, but this is in most cases impracticable. Therefore, put a clear description in your register, such as 'Worcester coffee can' or 'Original photograph, about 1914: group of soldiers', with the customer's estimate of the value beside it. Then keep the register as far away from the articles as possible so that, in the event of fire, the two are not lost together.

Because some customers may forget that, or where, they have left a clock or other article for repair, it is wise to be sure that you have an address or telephone number where you can contact the owner. Perhaps ask also for a deposit or payment in advance. In repair work, there is a greater risk of people failing to collect their possessions, and you would be left with the loss not only of the cost of the materials you used but of the time expended—which you are unlikely to be able to recover even if, eventually, you sell the uncollected object.

bicycles

If there is an increasing number of cyclists in your area and you are reasonably handy, it could be profitable to set up a bicycle repair business. This can be done without needing more than a cupboard for tools and spare parts, and a shed or a yard or other suitable space where you can dismantle and reassemble bikes. You may need to stable some bikes overnight or for a few days while working on them, so a lockable covered bicycle rack or a lock-up shed could be useful, too. The tools required are relatively simple, plus oil, grease, paint, chrome cleaner, inner tubes and puncture repair equipment; some spare parts may be obtainable only from the bicycle's manufacturer.

Identify each bike carefully with its owner. Try to give some idea of how much you will charge for the job beforehand; it may be wise to ask for a deposit, particularly if you are at all doubtful about the bike being claimed when ready.

Tell local schools, colleges and clubs, firms and factories, that you are offering this service; also put notices in papers, shop windows, at your own premises.

If you have the necessary skill (and sources of supplies), rebuilding and restoring old, broken-down bicycles for resale can be profitable.

book binding

To acquire sufficient knowledge and skill to do book binding or book restoring on a commercial basis, you must attend classes. (A professional book binder has to serve a 5-year apprenticeship.)

There are a number of books on the subject, but many of them are now out of print so you may have to go to your local library for them. *Basic Bookbinding*, for example, by A W Lewis (£1.35, Dover Publications, distributed by Constable and Co) gives a good idea of the work involved and could be used on its own as a guide or in conjunction with an adult education class.

Presses are expensive and a secondhand basic set of brass tools for lettering a book will set you back about £25 (about £45 new) and you will need several of different sizes.

Do not embark on leather bindings until you have gained enough experience. It is probably the most profitable area of book binding but it is also the most expensive. Good leathers cost several pounds a square foot and you need to have a wide selection in order to match material you are repairing. Cloth and buckram (strong linen) are cheaper and easier to work.

Secondhand booksellers and dealers may welcome someone who can carry out anything from minor repairs to re-binding a book. Advertise locally and also in specialist or professional publications whose readers may want to have bound their reports, magazines or theses. Make sure to add return postage to your charge for any work you get by post.

Your charges must cover your overheads and your own time as well as the materials you use. Before spending too much time on a book which in itself is not worth more than a few pounds, get the customer's confirmation that he is willing to pay your price. Where there is a choice of material, you could then discuss the possibility of using a cheaper one.

china

China repair and restoration requires exceptional patience and an eye for detail, particularly in the moulding of replacements for missing pieces of porcelain. You need to have a gift for this painstaking, slow and complex work. Do not take on high quality work until you have gained adequate experience.

Courses on this subject are sometimes run by local authority adult institutes. Details of some courses on china mending for beginners are available from Robin Hood's Workshop, 18 Bourne Street, Sloane Square, London SW1. West Dean College at Chichester, West Sussex, has residential courses on china restoration, and there are short courses at other residential colleges in different parts of the country.

You need good light to work by, with very good ventilation and freedom from dust and grease. After an initial outlay of a couple of hundred pounds for drill, air brush and compressor, the running costs for materials are low. But you will need the best quality sable brushes; these do not wear well and are expensive to replace. The small knives, methylated spirits, contact adhesive you use, and the china being mended, should be kept safely out of the way of other members of the household, especially children and pets.

Try advertising your services in the local paper, and ask the local museum or antique shops whether they can put work in your way. If a customer should bring work that is obviously of outstanding quality, consider referring him to the Victoria and Albert Museum or some other place where specialist knowledge would be forthcoming.

clocks

Interest in the mechanism of clocks is not enough to set yourself up to do watch and clock repairing; you have to have some aptitude as well and some training. You could take one of the six-month graded correspondence courses in technical horology offered by the British Horological Institute (Upton Hall, Upton, Newark, Notts NG23 5TE) and an advanced one-year course in antique clock restoration at West Dean College, Chichester, West Sussex. Some technical colleges and adult institutes have classes on clock making and repairing.

You will need good light to work by and an assortment of spare parts, obtainable from specialist suppliers. It is possible to pick up discarded clocks and watches at junk shops, auctions, jumble sales, to cannibalise for their parts—or, where possible, repair, restore and sell.

When you feel sufficiently experienced, you could offer your freelance repair services to local jewellers.

The intricacy of each job and the time it therefore takes will be the main criterion for the price you charge.

picture framing

To do picture mounting and framing to a professional standard, you need knowledge of what you are doing, skill, and a lot of space. The minimum area to work in and for storage of materials would be, say, that of a double garage.

Tools are expensive, particularly the implement for cutting mitred corners (without this, the corners will not be good enough—and a frame with wrong corners is not worth any money at all). To be able to offer to make any size and kind of frame, you will need a selection of mouldings for each type of frame suitable for different styles of picture and a selection within each group (gold, plain wood, antique finish, metal and so on). Having a wide choice enables you to offer alternatives at different prices.

Glass and hardboard come in large sheets (approx 6 ft × 4 ft) which are difficult to handle, and need to be cut to size. Outside London, materials may not be readily available, and firms do not usually sell in small quantities, so some capital is needed to stock up. Before committing yourself financially, try to find out what demand there is in your area and whether people are prepared to pay an economic price.

Try advertising, and getting work through a local craft or book shop, art gallery, photographer, artists' group; tell architects and designers, advertising agencies, and local firms or institutions that you can do framing for them.

Upholstery

Even if you have done some upholstery for yourself and friends, you should consider improving your skill before asking for money for doing it. Local authorities run upholstery classes at adult education institutes. Courses can be taken for a City and Guilds certificate and for a National Federation of Women's Institutes basic certificate. There are other long and short courses at various colleges throughout the country, including the London College of Furniture.

Reference books are of particular importance; even when you have attended evening classes, there will be many occasions when instant referral to a book will be essential.

It might be better to start on one type of furniture and concentrate on that rather than to diversify, particularly into more complicated work.

Collecting and housing and delivering large pieces of furniture, such as settees and armchairs, may be a problem unless you have an estate car or a van. Also, you will need plenty of space for working on the larger pieces. Some heavy pieces of furniture demand considerable physical strength not only for loading and unloading but also moving around when working on them.

It may be worth getting public liability insurance cover for any injury or damage caused to customers or others when handling and delivering furniture.

You probably already possess quite a few tools, but you may have to buy more or extra equipment: special needles, shears or very sharp scissors, web stretcher. You may need a heavy duty sewing machine if your domestic one cannot cope with thicknesses of material.

Often, when the covering is removed from furniture, defects in the wood frame are revealed. Be prepared to have to get the necessary repairs done before re-upholstering.

Some customers may want you to advise them on choosing the fabric for the covering, so, as well as developing an eye for colour and design in furnishing schemes, you need to acquire some knowledge of the characteristics and suitability of the various materials, particularly the synthetic fibres that are used nowadays. You can get samples of covering materials from manufacturers, but most of them charge quite a lot if you ask for a range of sample patterns. Manufacturers generally only allow a discount on covering materials if a guaranteed amount is purchased in any one year. If there is an upholsterers' warehouse locally, it may have a wide stock of materials and braids, and may be willing to supply you on a trade basis.

Be careful to be accurate about how much material is needed for each job, so that you are not caught with too little or too much. It is important when measuring material to remember the direction of the nap: it can make a considerable difference to the amount of material needed for the nap to run in the correct direction throughout the piece. If the customer is doing the measuring, give precise instructions about the measurements to be taken, with a sketch where necessary. This applies to measuring for curtains and loose covers, too.

Remember to point out to your customers (at least, the first time you do a job) that, even if they provide the covering fabric, additional materials have to be used for the under covering and stuffing, and that you will have to buy braid, buttons or other finishing items, for which you will be charging as well as for your time on the job. When you do so, show these items separately on the bill, and perhaps attach receipts.

Be careful about the timing of orders. Always assume that things will take a lot longer than you think and therefore do not make any rash promises about the time any job is likely to take you. Do not accept two large items at the same time unless you have plenty of space and time to cope. Your machining and hammering may disturb neighbours and your household, so you may have to restrict that stage of the work to a limited number of daytime hours.

In secondhand shops, antique shops and markets you may find attractive pieces of furniture in need of re-upholstering. A few hours' hard work can transform a dirty old chair into a beautiful piece of furniture. A knowledge of the right braid and materials to go with the period of the piece is important, and learning how to clean and polish show-wood on antique furniture will be useful. To sell something you have re-covered or re-upholstered, you may have to go to the expense of advertising —perhaps in the local newspaper or one of the specialist magazines.

Writing

In order to make money from writing, it is important to write for a specific market and to produce what is acceptable to editors and publishers.

Before sending out anything (perhaps even before you begin to write), study the market to discover where to send your work. The *Writers' and Artists' Yearbook* (A & C Black Ltd, 1979 edition £2.25) contains information about magazines, newspapers, publishers, literary agents, markets for plays, tips on copyright, tax, correction of proofs, typing services.

If you are planning a novel, note which publishers deal with the type you have in mind. It is easier to break into print if your novel can be categorised: thriller, historical, western, romance, gothic, science fiction. You may find it hard to persuade any publisher to risk his money on an experimental novel.

For a full-length book, send a synopsis and a sample chapter first. For short stories, articles and features, establish the length, subject matter, taboos, and check the editor's requirements in the *W & A Yearbook*. Some editors and publishers, if requested, will send you guidelines on what they want.

The BBC and ITV accept stories, scripts and plays from outside contributors, and so do local radio stations. For tv serials, it is not necessary to write the entire serial before you submit it. A synopsis and sample episode are enough. Scripts should be typed with 'sound' down the centre of the page and 'action' down the right hand side. Remember to time the work carefully, and to allow for commercial breaks if you are writing for ITV. *Writing for the BBC* (75p), a guide for professional and part-time freelance writers on possible markets for their work within the BBC, is available from BBC Publications, 35 Marylebone High Street, London W1M 4AA.

Most editors and publishers will not even consider a hand-written piece of work, so it is essential to have a typewriter capable of producing at least one legible carbon copy. Otherwise, you will have to rely on typing services, which will be expensive. Evolve some sort of filing system immediately, and keep details of all work sent out, to whom, date, reply. And keep a careful note (and receipts) of any expenses that might be allowable for tax, such as paper, postage, fares, telephone calls, reference books.

Type on one side of the paper only, use double spacing and leave adequate margins at the sides and top. Put your name and address on the title page. Check any special requirements of publisher or editor and follow them precisely.

Send the top copy (and keep the carbon copy) and a stamped self-addressed envelope. If the typescript comes back looking tatty, it is worth retyping at least the title page and first few pages before sending it off to another editor.

Getting a verdict on a script may take up to 6 months (book publishers' average time is around 2 months). Try not to write impatient letters; the manuscript may have to be vetted by several readers. But if you do not hear after a couple of months, write a gentle reminder.

Be prepared not to be told the reason for a rejection. Editors and publishers generally do not go into explanations. However, a rejection slip does not necessarily mean that your work is no good. Try it elsewhere.

When a work is accepted, the author may be asked to proof-read it. The method of marking up the corrections to be made is given in detail in the *W & A Yearbook*. You may be charged for a percentage of corrections due to your mistakes or second thoughts.

Writing is a lonely business. If possible, try to have some regularity in working hours: exclude other things and be firm with friends, and the family, who think that because you are at home they can interrupt you at any time or ask you to do tasks for them.

Various writers' associations are listed in the *W & A Yearbook*. There may be special enrolment conditions, such as the prospective member being a published, or about to be published, writer.

The Society of Authors (84 Drayton Gardens, London SW10 9SD), which is an independent trades union, gives individual members legal and business advice on matters affecting their rights as authors, and has established specialist groups such as the educational writers' group and the children's writers' group. It has a broadcasting committee which negotiates on behalf of writers in radio, and advises on individual agreements in television, theatre and films.

The Writers' Guild of Great Britain (430 Edgware Road, London W2 1EH), affiliated to the TUC, negotiates agreements for writers of films, stories, books, television, radio and stage plays. It represents writers and gives advice to members on contracts and earnings, and professional status.

Read carefully an initial letter of acceptance, which will outline the general terms of the contract, and be sure you know what rights you are selling. Do not sign anything presented to you—especially any agreement—until you have read and understood it and perhaps had it vetted by your writers' society. If you have an agent, he will vet the contract for you.

Do not sell all your rights unless you are desperate for money (or to see your work in print). If you do sell the copyright, you disclaim all ownership and your work may be used again and again without your receiving another penny for it.

For short stories, in the first instance offer first british serial rights. This gives the magazine the right to print your story only once. Then you can find another market for the same story, offering second rights.

In the case of a book, if you are offered a lump sum without mention of royalties, ask for royalties—that is, a percentage of sales. A common arrangement is to get a lump sum as an advance on royalties. This sum is usually split—say, half on signing the contract and half on publication. You may not get much from your first book, but your first contract sets the pattern for future ones. Bear in mind translation and overseas rights (the american market is the most lucrative), paperback versions, adaptation for television, radio, film.

A literary agent may be able to negotiate better terms for you if you are too shy to haggle for yourself, and, particularly with short pieces, may know of markets which you have failed to take into account. It can be as difficult to find an agent who will take you on as it is to find a publisher, so if an agent accepts your work, you can congratulate yourself. You may have to pay an initial reading fee and the agent will deduct 10 to 15 per cent from your earnings.

indexing

For indexing, unlike writing, you do not have to have a talent but must be logical and methodical in your thinking and able to face the challenge of making information contained in books and periodicals easily retrievable. Relatively few indexers are directly employed by publishers. Specialist knowledge of the subject-matter of a publication is much more important for an indexer than familiarity with the world of publishing. The majority of successful indexers are subject-specialists in one or more fields, at least to graduate or equivalent level.

It is useful to have your own typewriter, a set of basic reference books and a quiet room to work in.

Work may be spasmodic. It is usual to charge by the hour rather than by the number of entries or pages, or by a lump sum. Joining the Society of Indexers (secretary at 28 Johns Avenue, London NW4 4EN) will keep you in touch with other indexers and indexing generally through *The Indexer*, the Society's twice-yearly journal, and the newsletter. Once you are established, you can apply to be on the classified register of approved indexers whom authors and publishers can contact.

CRAFTWORK

When making use of a creative manual talent, it is no good expecting to sell the work of your hands unless you have reached a high degree of skill and can produce to a consistent standard. In many cases, you will be competing with established professionals so, if you want to be taken seriously, you will have to aim to attain a similar standard and not to approach the work as a dabbler doing just for fun what is another person's basic livelihood.

Given a good and cooperative tutor and some application on your part, doing a course in your particular subject should enable you to bring yourself up from good amateur status to a near-professional level where you can confidently ask other people to pay for your products.

For information on classes and part-time and full-time courses, first write to your local education authority; local craft societies also give information on courses, and a list of arts centres is available from the Arts Council of Great Britain, 105 Piccadilly, London W1V 0AU.

If you can afford more time than local further education classes, you may profit from a concentrated course at a residential college. For instance, West Dean College, Chichester, West Sussex, is concerned with art and craft education and the training of skilled practitioners. The residential courses cover a wide range of creative and practical subjects; some courses on restoration work run for a year, others are from one to ten days.

The National Institute of Adult Education publishes a six-monthly calendar (50p from 19B de Montfort Street, Leicester LE1 7GH) giving details of residential short courses at colleges in England and Wales.

The Department of Education and Science (Elizabeth House, York Road, London SE1 7PH) can give information about relevant government-backed organisations, including:

Crafts Council

---

12 Waterloo Place, London SW1Y 4AU
The Crafts Council administers the government grant allocated annually for the crafts in England and Wales. It provides grants, loans and bursaries to craftsmen under various schemes, to help them maintain and improve their standards, become better known to the public and sell their work. It holds regular exhibitions of work by artist craftsmen at its Waterloo Place gallery and manages the craft shop at the Victoria and Albert Museum. An information service is available on craft courses, craft shops and galleries, exhibitions. Amongst its publications is one on setting up a workshop.

Federation of British Craft Societies

---

43 Earlham Street, London WC2H 9LD
The FBCS represents specialist societies and guilds, and national and regional multi-craft societies. It receives a grant from the Crafts Council to enable it to promote the work of member societies and represent the craft professions. It publishes a quarterly *Newsletter* publicising members' activities, and offers information on courses and other activities for craftsmen.

British Crafts Centre

---

43 Earlham Street, London WC2H 9LD
The BCC is an independent, non-profit-making body, financed by members' subscriptions, by commissions on sales, and by a grant from the Crafts Council. Exhibitions are held in its gallery, including a biennial members' exhibition. Membership is open to all, not only practising craftsmen.

The Council of Regional Arts Associations (CORAA)

The fifteen regional arts associations in England and Wales are most active in promoting the crafts by organising craft centres and touring craft exhibitions; some provide bursaries for artists and craftsmen. Details of each regional association's activities are given in the publication *Arts with the people*, available free from the Department of Education and Science.

Wales Craft Council

Ladywell House, Park Street, Newtown, Powys SY16 1JB
The WCC, which is sponsored by the Welsh Development Agency and the Development Board for Rural Wales, encourages and promotes the manufacture, sale and distribution of all craft products manufactured within Wales. Full-time craftsmen who register (no charge) with the WCC can get advice on design, product development, promotion and marketing, and are listed in the guide which is circulated to buyers in this country and abroad.

Scottish Development Agency crafts section

102 Telford Road, Edinburgh EH4 2NP
The crafts section within the small business division of the SDA, in association with a crafts consultative committee, helps scottish craftsmen by giving practical advice, offering grants and loans for workshops and training schemes, maintaining an index of craftworkers, organising an annual crafts trade fair.

Council for Small Industries in Rural Areas (CoSIRA)

Queen's House, Fish Row, Salisbury, Wiltshire SP1 1EX
CoSIRA, a government-financed organisation operating in England only, can provide technical and management advice and, in certain cases, make loans to small manufacturing and servicing concerns, for rural crafts and tourist accommodation.

finding outlets

It would be useful to talk to as many people as possible who are doing the same type of work or are similarly freelance, to gain from their experiences and know-how.

Once you have achieved a high level of technical competence, you should aim to sell not only to customers' individual orders but through general outlets such as craft shops and market stalls, or from your own premises. Perhaps a bookshop or teashop, or a hotel in a holiday area, will allow you to have a small display case of your wares in the shop or foyer or entrance room. Try to ensure that the things are properly displayed and clearly identifiable as yours. Attach your name and address wherever possible.

The Women's Institutes' cooperative market scheme covers hand-made craftwork as well as prepared food and preserves, and is not restricted to WI members. The markets are held, usually for one morning a week, in towns and villages accessible to rural producers. The money from the sale of the goods goes back to the producer, less a commission of 10 to 15 per cent deducted for running expenses.

The WI markets are subject to the usual trading regulations, and goods are sold at reasonable prices according to the locality. Men and women who are not WI members may apply to become shareholders for 5p and can then sell their produce through the markets, provided it comes up to the high standard required. Some markets which do not normally sell crafts do so for a limited period before Christmas and Easter.

You can find out whether there is a WI market in your county, and get further information on markets, from the market adviser, National Federation of Women's Institutes, 39 Eccleston Street, London SW1W 9NT (send a stamped addressed envelope with your request).

An entry in the CoSIRA book of *Craft workshops in the english countryside* should be a good boost to your business. Application should be made about the middle of the year for the following year's edition. Someone from CoSIRA will come to visit you and look at your premises and wares. There is an annual fee for an entry (£6 for 1979). You can use the book in reverse and find out from it where there are retail craft shops and the type of work they accept for sale. Similarly, in Scotland an entry can be paid for in the visitors' guide to craftshops and the retailers' directory of craftsmen, issued by the crafts section of the SDA. A craftworker in Scotland can apply for membership of the Scottish Craft Centre (Acheson House, 140 Canongate, Edinburgh EH8 8DD) and, if accepted, can have work displayed at the Centre.

But without previous experience in selling your wares, it can be difficult to get going. You may need to adjust your approach to other people to allow for the different relationship of seller and buyer, amateur and professional, customer and agent. You will need perhaps to be a little tougher in your approach, while remaining aware of the other person's criteria and needs. When trying to get a retailer to buy your products to sell in his shop, remember that his need is to satisfy his eventual customer, not you.

When you go into a shop to sell, have a definite idea of the price you want for your products. The price you ask depends on whether your articles are going to be bought by the shop for resale, or sold for you on commission. If the latter, your figure should allow for the deduction.

Be attentive to the retailer's reactions, comment and advice. For instance, he may like your products but not be able to display them easily, or may want them wrapped. A simple display unit could set off the work attractively: say, a shelf or some dowling rods or hooks on a board. Some handicrafts need no wrapping or labels, others are much improved when in appropriate packaging and labelled. Packaging needs to be in keeping with the character of the handicraft, and may need to be transparent. Labels must always be neat. Printed peel-off sticky labels can be useful, or a carefully written label with the craftsman's name adds a personal touch.

A resurgence of fashionable interest in hand-made goods has meant that there is a market for well made garments and items such as patchwork cushions and covers, quilts, macramé plant-pot holders, woven baskets and rushwork, embroidery. With these and similar pastimes, the major investment is in the labour. Cost this in as realistically as you can when estimating for a commissioned article. When you are making to sell generally, rather than to a specific order, keep a note of the time a particular piece of work has taken you, so that you can add a suitable amount to the cost of the materials when working out a price to charge. You will have to set an arbitrary value on your own time: a realistic one might price your work out of the ordinary buyer's reach and you would have to depend on the very rich discriminating enthusiast.

Offer to give a demonstration of your skill at local meetings of social or art groups—not to earn money there but to publicise yourself, show how good you are and get orders and recommendations.

Another outlet, once you are good enough, would be to give classes yourself in your subject. This might help to pay for equipment you need, as well as spreading the word about your skill and enterprise. Glass engraving, jewellery making, book binding and such like could be taught at home to amateurs.

supplies

There are mail order suppliers specialising in materials for handicrafts. For instance, Fred Aldous Ltd (PO BOX 135, 37 Lever Street, Manchester M60 1UX) and Dryad (PO BOX 38, Northgates, Leicester LE1 9BU) have illustrated catalogues of a wide range of materials, including for flower and jewellery making, basketry, chair caning, candle making, embroidery and needlecraft, enamelling, leather work, macramé, paperwork, picture making, pottery, tapestry, stonecraft, and also offer a selection of books and leaflets on handwork subjects. The Dryad catalogue costs about £1.50.

Some manual crafts require plenty of space for equipment or the work. You may need a greater variety and range of materials than when you were doing the work as a hobby. Without being needlessly extravagant, do not stint on the quality of materials you buy. (You can claim a tax allowance for items used for business or commercial purposes.) Some equipment may be available secondhand—but check its condition carefully.

Candle making

There are several ways of producing candles, some fairly simple, each giving different results. You can learn how to make the different kinds by buying a kit in a craft shop (rather expensive) and studying the instructions, or teaching yourself by trial and error with the help of books such as *Simple methods of candle manufacture* (75p from Intermediate Technology Publications Ltd, 9 King Street, London WC2E 8HN).

In addition to wax, stearin, dyes, and wicks of the right size, you need moulds, either improvised or specially bought, a frame for dipping, vessels for the prepared wax. The process may be a bit messy until you are skilled, and takes up a fair amount of space for preparing vats of different colours, stacking the moulds or letting the candles hang while the wax solidifies.

The ingredients used carry a high fire risk; inform your insurers and be prepared for your premium to be increased. Be careful not to let the wax and stearin overheat when melting: it can flare up like overheated cooking fat. If you sell candles in candleholders, make sure that the candleholders are not made of a flammable material (plastic is not suitable).

Glass engraving

For glass engraving you need considerable skill in drawing and designing, otherwise you have to use other people's designs. Talent as an artist is the first requirement; then a steady hand. If you make a mistake, you may have to begin again on another glass; it is expensive to have mistakes polished out.

A few further education colleges and institutes have courses on glass engraving. The Guild of Glass Engravers (43 Earlham Street, London WC2H 9LD) is open to lay and craft members. All those practising engraving must join as craft members and can participate in the exhibitions organised by the Guild. Its quarterly journal includes information about techniques.

The Guild has published a comprehensive primer *Starting from scratch* (£3, for members) with full details of the glass and equipment for the various techniques.

Glass (or crystal) varies in quality according to the lead content: the lower the lead content, the harder to engrave. Ordinary glass brought to you by a customer for engraving may not be suitable for proper engraving.

As well as allowing for your time and skill, your charges will have to vary according to whether you or your customer supplies the basic glass article. A popular line is to engrave pieces of table glass with initials and/or dates for special anniversaries. Emblems for societies or pictures of houses may also be commissioned as gifts; these may need to be adapted for engraving techniques.

Jewellery

A wide range of decorative jewellery can be made at home from natural ingredients. For example, stones you pick up can be polished in a tumbling machine (this is quite noisy and needs to be kept on for a long time; put it on in an unused room, or garage). Precious stones can be bought from jewellers—some have a more interesting range than others so it is worth shopping around; semi-precious and other stones can also be bought from craft shops.

You can buy blanks, mounts, clasps, chains, thread, quite cheaply from handicraft suppliers.

Before laying out a lot on materials or equipment of your own, experiment and find out in what technique you are most skilled to try to make money out of it. There are adult education courses on jewellery making and a City and Guilds certificate course in silversmiths' and allied crafts and jewellery.

gold and silver

Hatton Garden in London is an area particularly richly endowed with jewellers, dealers, merchants in metals and gems, and would be worth a special visit to find out about supplies of equipment and materials.

Silver, in sheets, can be bought without restriction from a bullion dealer; it is sold according to weight.

To buy gold, you have to have a licence from the Bank of England; there is no fee for this. For a fineness of 9 carat or below you need to complete application form G9 at the suppliers (a bank or bullion dealer). For gold of a higher caratage, it is necessary to submit application form GIP2 to the Bank of England via your own bank. Approval is normally given for gold for industrial purposes (that includes making jewellery) to applicants who have considerable experience in the use of precious metals. Most authorised dealers in gold keep a supply of application forms, or you can get one from the Exchange Control Notices and Forms Supply Counter, Bank of England, New Change, London EC4M 9AA.

Any item made of gold or silver or platinum in this country has to be hallmarked if it is to be sold by way of trade or business. (Tiny items—for example, in gold less than 1 gram in weight, in silver less than 7.78 grams—can be sold without a hallmark.) The article has to be sent to an assay office for testing. There are four in the UK:

The Assay Office
  Goldsmiths' Hall, Gutter Lane, London EC2V 8AQ
  Newhall Street, Birmingham B3 1SB
  137 Portobello Street, Sheffield S1 4DR
  15 Queen Street, Edinburgh EH2 1JE

A sample is taken from the article for analysis, preferably

before the final polishing, to check the purity of the metal: there are standards for the permissible proportion of alloyed metals.

You have to register your sponsor's mark, which is a design showing your initials, and pay a fee of £16.20. Thereafter, you are charged according to the type or weight of each article you submit for hallmarking. The complete hallmark consists of the sponsor's mark, the standard mark (denoting that the precious metal content of the alloy is not less than the appropriate standard), the mark of the assay office where the article has been tested (each has its own symbol) and the date letter for the year.

The assay offices issue a free booklet on hallmarks (send a stamped addressed 4 in × 9 in envelope). You can apply by post for information about getting your own products hallmarked, or go in person to the assay office to discuss the registration of your mark and to be told about the procedure for submitting articles for hallmarking there.

Pottery

Quite a lot of equipment is needed, and space for it. Do not go ahead and buy pottery equipment until you have attended a course or received advice from an instructor, or talked with a professional potter, or at least studied some books on the subject—otherwise you may find you have bought useless equipment. Even secondhand wheels are quite expensive.

An electric kiln is simplest for a beginner. A very small (3 kW) kiln can be run off an ordinary household electricity supply; you can use it on the white meter or economy tariff. A gas fired or a wood kiln requires more experience and closer attention when firing, but more interesting results are likely to be obtained.

You can buy a variety of ready-mixed clays from potter's merchants; it is proportionately cheaper the more you order at a time, so as much floor area as possible for storing it will be useful. Clay keeps well in the heavy-duty polythene sacks it is sold in.

The chemicals used for making up glazes can be a health hazard, so wipe up any spilt powder immediately and avoid touching or breathing it. Similarly, dust from dried clay can cumulatively become a hazard: do not brush it off but wipe with a damp cloth and keep the atmosphere moist.

Perhaps you can use an outside shed or empty garage as your workroom but it must have a sink and electric sockets. You will need a solid work surface and shelving.

If working in the home means limited space, the scale of pottery has to fit this. Small porcelain pieces can be made up with other simple materials, such as beads, wood and string to produce necklaces, bracelets, windchimes. Dolls' house crockery or dolls' teasets, little animals and ornaments sell for high prices, provided they are carefully made. Very little space is needed to produce this kind of work, and a sack of clay goes a long way.

In costing your work, allow for a high failure rate: with even a skilled potter, cracks sometimes appear during the firing.

If you join the Craftsmen Potters Association (William Blake House, Marshall Street, London W1V 1FD) as an associate or (if your work is of an acceptably high standard) as a full member, you can share information and interests with other potters, through the bi-monthly magazine *Ceramic Review*. Full members can exhibit and sell their work at William Blake House. The association publishes a directory of the work of full members, and has other publications and equipment available from its shop.

Soft toys and dolls

To extend or perfect your technique, an adult education course on toymaking, puppet making, carpentry, pattern cutting and similar subjects may be useful; there is a City and Guilds certificate in toymaking. Various television series deal with the subject.

When you are producing hand-made toys, you must be sure to make them safe toys—eyes well sewn in, no metal parts that could protrude, non-flammable materials.

Toys have to conform to the Toys (Safety) Regulations 1974 (SI 1367; from HMSO, 9p), the enforcement of which lies with the local authority. There is no active policing or inspection of premises, but if a customer complains of a hazard, trading standards officers or environmental health officers have the right to prosecute if a dangerous toy—that is, one not conforming to the Regulations—is being made.

A good guide to the legal requirements is the British Standards Institution's *Code for toys and playthings* (BS 3443, £3 from BSI, 101 Pentonville Road, London N1 9ND). More advanced and detailed, covering a wider range of playthings, is BS 5665 *Safety of toys*, which relates to future legislation. Stuffing materials should comply for cleanliness with BS 1425; if you just need a

small quantity of stuffing, you could buy a cheap pillow and use the filling because, legally, this must comply with the standard. The filling should be non-flammable, and so should the covering.

The BSI Test House (telephone 0442-3111) will test toys for eye security and give a general flammability report (fee from about £20), if you want the assurance of a professional test.

Animals or dolls can be life-like or fantasy beings. If you invent a creature, you may be on to a best seller. But do not waste your time making existing television characters: these are copyright and can only be reproduced under licence.

Materials need not cost you much, but you will need space for your sewing machine, for cutting out, and to store bags of stuffing and other bulky materials. Making—and putting on—clothes for dolls and animals is time-consuming but undressable toys are generally popular so you can charge extra for the extra time they take.

Dolls' clothes for specific sizes of dolls (choose ones which are widely sold) can be a good line to sell by post. Make them in pretty materials with a small pattern.

Another popular line, provided you have neat fingers and good eyesight, is dolls' house furniture, or even a complete dolls' house on commission. (Make sure the paints you use are non-toxic.) These can be collectors' items as much as toys and have to be of a very high standard of craftsmanship.

Whatever type of toy you make, the best selling time will be in the weeks leading up to Christmas. Make sure that you have a good supply then—even if it means that you have to borrow for the extra outlay. You may have to enlist helpers or out-workers temporarily.

NEW VENTURES

There are many money-making outlets for anyone who is energetic and organised, even without a previous skill or training, such as selling for others, keeping animals, looking after children. Choose something in which you have an interest and which you are likely to enjoy and therefore do well.

Some occupations may not earn you a lot of money on their own,but could be combined with another so that together they provide you with a reasonable amount. For instance, telephone selling could be fitted in with being a mail order agent, hiring out equipment with taking lodgers, beekeeping with rearing goats. But some occupations are too time-consuming to allow a dual role, so you have to ensure that you can make enough at the one activity to bring you the money you need or want.

Selling for others

Some firms use freelance agents rather than shops and employees to sell their products, and may need new recruits in your area.

corset agent

This is a job for women only. Corset manufacturers advertise locally when they want agents (sometimes called consultants) or you could write direct to a company such as Spirella to ask whether they need someone in your area. If you are accepted, you will be trained by a representative of the company to measure customers correctly and will be told what the manufacturer can provide and how to sell it (your contract will preclude you from working for more than one manufacturer). There is usually a fee (of about £20) for the training and for stationery and advertising material and an initial supply of garments to display to customers. The fee may be refunded once you have· placed a certain number of orders.

You measure the customer, send in detailed specifications to the manufacturer who makes up the required garment accordingly and lets you buy it at the wholesale price. You sell to your customer at whatever price you choose. If you make a mistake in the specification after the first few months, or the customer changes her mind, you (or the customer) have to pay for the alterations to put it right; if the manufacturer gets it wrong, you are not charged for the necessary alterations. But you may have to be able to prove where the fault lay.

You must take accurate measurements and keep proper records. There is paperwork and some book-keeping involved. You will have to keep an efficient appointments system and have a pleasant small room for fitting your clients where you are not interrupted. You are likely to need a lot of patience and tact, because women are going to consult you in order to avoid having to deal with conventional saleswomen in a shop. Some clients will prefer you to go to them, but you can try to make this the exception rather than the norm. It is up to you how much or how little you work, and how much profit you make.

A snag is that a satisfied customer may not need to return for a year or more for a new corset, so you will have to find new customers all the time. Make use of the corset manufacturer's promotion material and advertise yourself locally as providing a service for foundation garments, bras, corselets, girdles, corsets. Try health clinics, fashion shops, hairdressers.

mail order agent

Many women in this country use mail order catalogues from various firms to buy goods for their families through the firm's local agent. Paying by weekly instalments is a basic feature of this form of retailing.

An agent is paid commission by the mail order firm on the orders he or she sends in: 10 per cent in cash or the equivalent of 12½ per cent if taken in goods. You cannot earn much at it because there is a limit to the amount your 'customers' will spend. Even £500-worth of business is only £50 a year for the agent.

To become an agent, you can write to a mail order company, or fill in a coupon in a newspaper or circular that has been delivered to your home. If you can cope with the work, particularly the paperwork, you can be agent for two or three firms (but most of the catalogues are very similar). You would have to make sure that you keep their accounts separate.

First, you get the catalogue and the stationery the firm provides. Some mail order firms send a sales representative to deliver the catalogue. With your first order, you have to send in some personal details. At the beginning, you will not be allowed more than about £10 or £15 credit for each of your customers but when you are established as an agent, the amount of credit available to you increases. If you do not send in orders, the company may send you persuasive letters and eventually perhaps ask for its catalogue back.

The things you order for other people are usually delivered to you; bulky items may be delivered direct to the customer. You have to deal with any returns or replacements needed but the mail order company pays the costs. It is up to you to arrange how and when to deliver the goods to the buyer and get the money owed each week; you are expected to pay the weekly amounts to the mail order firm regularly. You must be prepared to be firm with your clients and not let them fall behind with their payments. If any customer gets into arrears with payments and you are unable to deal with the situation, you can refer the problem to the company which then takes action.

You must keep an accurate record of your customers' orders to you, and when you passed them on to the mail order company. Some of the paperwork seems unnecessary but do not dispose of records even if you stop using a particular firm: there may be queries and problems long after you have closed your accounts. If the mail order company's system goes wrong— and it does happen—you must have clear and accurate records to rely on. The company may make mistakes in sending the wrong articles, not sending articles, claiming goods returned have not been and taking weeks to send the goods ordered.

You are likely to have quite a lot of money and valuable goods on your premises at times, so you should check your insurance cover and have a suitable place for keeping cash and items until you can get them out of the house.

The Mail Order Traders' Association has issued a code of practice to which its members should adhere and which lays down their responsibilities to the public and to agents. The code, which includes a list of member firms, is available from the Association, 507 Corn Exchange Building, Fenwick Street, Liverpool L2 7RA.

selling party organiser

A wide variety of products get sold through parties—jewellery, clothes, household equipment (Tupperware has always been sold in this way). A good way of getting a feel of the type of approach needed is to get yourself invited to one of these parties and, at the end of it, talk to the organiser.

A party organiser does not have to give all the parties herself but is committed to organising a certain number of parties a week which she has to persuade people to give. The organiser is expected to attend the parties to talk about or demonstrate the product and encourage orders. You are given an initial training course and usually have to be prepared to go along to refresher sessions to be kept up-to-date with latest products and developments.

You get paid a commission of around 20 per cent of the cash value of sales from the firm supplying the goods, or take the difference between the price the customer pays for the goods and what you have to pay the firm for them. Make sure you understand how the firm's commission or payment system works before signing anything when you are being taken on. Check whether there are any other incidentals, such as promotional leaflets, samples, or gifts for the hostess, which you may have to pay for.

Paperwork and record keeping and some accounting are involved. Finding alternative hostesses and potential buyers (not just good party-goers) will be the most difficult part of the organiser's job. Generally, goods ordered at the party are delivered to the hostess and she collects and hands over the money for them.

The Direct Sales and Service Association (47 Windsor Road,

Slough, Berkshire SL1 2EE) represents the direct selling industry. Most firms selling through party plan and other in-home selling systems belong, and have to meet the standards which the DSSA requires from its members.

telephone selling

There are agencies who use people freelance to make a series of telephone calls on behalf of clients wanting to test the potential market for a product, get orders, make appointments for representatives to call, complete research questionnaires. A few individual firms may employ someone direct, but the work then is likely to be short-term and spasmodic; even the agencies cannot guarantee a constant workload.

A good voice and pleasant telephone manner are prerequisites, plus some quiet persistence and an interest in the challenge of having to respond to different personalities with each call. Even so, someone who has not had some experience of similar work with the telephone or of selling may not be accepted.

It may mean having another telephone installed or an extension or a plug-in system. It is possible to have an instrument that can be used only for outgoing calls. Ask your local telephone area office for leaflet DLX 4, which lists various telephone apparatus and charges, and find out what the possibilities and costs would be in your case.

You need to be able to site the telephone in a quiet part of the house, where you will not be interrupted, and where you can have plenty of space around for writing down answers or notes and completing order forms or questionnaires. You may find it helpful to have a device to hold the telephone handset, or even a headphone, so that your hands are free to write.

A clock with a clear second hand or a telephone timer (or even a stop watch) will be essential, so that you can monitor and charge for your calls accurately. And you will need all the relevant telephone directories for the districts you cover.

You are paid (something like 25p) for each call you make, sometimes more for longer or long distance calls. If you are employed direct, ask for a deposit to make sure that you will not have to meet a hefty telephone bill out of your own money.

data preparation

Firms or organisations who send out questionnaires often need outside help to prepare the information on the returned questionnaires for computer processing. This work can be done as an outworker under instruction from an agent, without necessarily having previous experience. It involves checking the content and continuity of the answers, sorting open-ended questions, adding coding references, and generally preparing the questionnaires for analysis by the computer.

You must be methodical, and will need adequate desk space, a large table and somewhere to store the questionnaires on which you are working. If they are not delivered and collected, the postage should be paid. The work is paid on an hourly basis or by consignment of questionnaires—which is more lucrative only if you are efficient and experienced.

To get work, you can ask firms listed in the telephone directory yellow pages as doing computer or data processing for the name and address of the agent(s) they use, and then ask the agent for work.

hiring out

It can be worthwhile investing in a quantity of things that people need occasionally, in order to hire them out. Examples are bicycles, prams and pushchairs (especially in a holiday area), jigsaw puzzles, power tools, sewing machines, lawn mowers and other household or garden equipment. Build up on your stock when you find out what is suitable and popular, such as bikes with a child's seat, perhaps.

You must have good quality stuff, to stand up to being handled (probably often mishandled) by people to whom it does not belong and who may therefore be less than careful with it.

If lending something mechanical or electrical, such as a lawn mower, it is as well to be able to do the maintenance and repairs yourself (the machines must be kept in tiptop condition); otherwise, your bill at the local repair shop or garage may eat up any proceeds from the hire charge.

Capital outlay may have to be high (six bicycles at one go) but you should get some immediate return. Your overheads involve mostly your own time on paperwork, and repairs. You must have a telephone to deal with enquiries and bookings.

You can set your own terms for length of hire, collection and delivery, charges for transport or postage, accessories or extras. It may be worth drawing up a formal hiring contract and getting it checked by a solicitor before putting it into operation.

Keep a careful record of who has hired what and when, due return dates, extras supplied (for instance, sander attachment), condition when taken.

Ask for a deposit large enough to cover the cost of the article should it not be brought back or brought back damaged. Or make a list of charges for any damage (for example, brake wire broken 40p, wheel buckled £2) and give a copy to the customer to avoid the embarrassment of having to refuse to return deposit money because of damage.

You should arrange with your insurers for cover for the extra equipment and machines you will have around on your premises (there may be an extra fire risk from some) and for your responsibility in case anyone else or their property gets damaged through its use. The insurers will probably want to establish that any equipment (especially mechanical or electrical) will be regularly serviced and maintained in good order, and that you provide adequate instructions for its use.

Advertise in newsagents' shops, the local paper, at welfare clinics and, if you are in a holiday area, through the regional tourist board's publicity.

collectors' items

Someone who has enjoyed collecting as a hobby may find that his or her collection can become the basis for a money-making trade, given the right contacts and knowledge of the particular field of collectors' items: stamps, coins, specialist books, thimbles, matchbox or cigarette cases, postcards and so on.

The advantage is that a lot of the exchanging and selling can be done from home, by advertising in specialist publications, and by postal circularisation. You have to build up a list of potential sellers and potential buyers—a slow business. Postage will be the major expense. And you will need to be able to go out every so often to markets, auctions, shops, other dealers, to augment and replenish your stock.

Boarding animals

Unless you live in a fairly isolated situation, this is a venture where you may run into trouble with the neighbours because of animal noises and smells. It would be wise to discuss your proposed arrangement in advance with your nearest neighbours, to get their agreement and cooperation; if asked, they are unlikely to say 'no'; if not asked, they are likely to grumble.

If you board cats or dogs for payment, you count as the keeper of an animal boarding establishment and come under the Animal Boarding Establishments Act 1963. This means that you must have a licence from your local authority. The annual fee, which is set by each local authority, is likely to be between £5 and £12. The application form and a notice giving details of the requirements are available from the local authority.

Particulars required on the application form include the number, construction and size of quarters in which animals will be accommodated, heating and lighting arrangements, method of ventilation, water supply, fire precautions, arrangements for food storage and for disposal of excreta, isolation facilities for the prevention and control of infectious disease. An inspector from the local authority will come to check the proposed accommodation, arrangements and precautions. You will have to keep a register of the animals' arrivals and departures open to inspection by the local authority inspector or authorised veterinary surgeon at any time.

You will need planning permission from the local authority for change of use of your premises, and also if you intend to build any runs or pens for the animals.

It is worth taking advice from a veterinary surgeon from the earliest stage. Looking after someone's cat while the owner is away on holiday for a week is very different to having to look after a variety of animals, with which you may not have had any dealings before and may not therefore be able to recognise warning signals of illness or distress. Veterinary fees must be taken into account, as must the time commitment.

You would be wise to have an arrangement with a local veterinary surgeon to come to deal with any accidents or illnesses. This works both ways: a vet is often asked to recommend a cattery or kennels.

Take out insurance for your liabilities. A block policy for boarding kennels and catteries such as the one offered by the Equine and Livestock Insurance Company, indemnifies you for legal liability to the owners of the animals and to third parties. The premium is calculated according to the number of animals you can board in your establishment. You can ask the animal's owner to pay for the cover that applies to the animal: loss by theft or straying, damage to other people or property caused by the animal, veterinary fees, compensation if the animal should die.

If you are keeping the animals in pens or cages outside, there will be quite a lot of cleaning out work to be done. It may be a good idea to have an extension bell for the telephone fixed outside the house, so that you hear it when out with the animals.

You have to decide whether you are willing to have any cat or dog in the house; if so, you may have to segregate incompatible boarders in different rooms or areas, which could be tricky.

Dogs will require exercising, not necessarily by taking them on walks, which is quite a responsibility. Provide an exercise area within your own ground where the dogs can be taken in turn a few times each day. You should not take on dogs unless you are an energetic person and like being frequently out of doors, regardless of the weather.

Set a basic scale for boarding charges and make clear what they cover in the way of food and accommodation, veterinary attention, and what any extras will be. In some cases, you may want to ask for a deposit.

Your appointments system must be foolproof and accurate about bookings in and out and times for delivery and collection. This is particularly important during the holiday season, including the long weekends; be careful not to overbook. (You will have to time your own holidays so as not to miss out on the peak boarding times.)

If you have young children in the household, find out before taking a dog whether it reacts well or aggressively to children, so that you can take any precautions that seem necessary. Find out whether a bitch is on heat or due to be. If so, you will have to be careful about taking male boarders at the same time, and will have to take precautions to keep neighbouring males away.

Never accept an animal with a hot nose, runny eyes, or any other obvious affliction. Ask for a vet's certificate of health if in any doubt. Get all details about the pet and its idiosyncracies, for instance about food, and any medicaments that may be required. Enquire when the animal was last vaccinated and against what diseases; ask the owner to bring vaccination certificates.

Take the address or telephone number of where the owners are, or of a friend or relative, to contact in case of emergency.

Make a note of any equipment owners bring for their pets, and mark it with some form of identification. Ask the owner to provide brushes and combs. This is a saving for you, and minimises the risk of transferring fleas.

Memorise the animal's name carefully, and get the owner to tell you what commands it responds to.

You may find that people call unexpectedly to have a look round, with a view to boarding their pet with you later, so try to keep the place looking orderly and welcoming at any reasonable time. A notice board beside the gate (for this, you may need planning permission) will help to guide prospective customers to your establishment.

other boarders

It is simpler to board small animals such as rabbits, gerbils, hamsters, caged birds and fish, which come in their own cages or aquaria. They can be kept in a suitable outbuilding: dry and draughtproof, with electricity if required for heating and aerating aquaria. Problems of compatability or exercise do not arise and there is less possibility of cross-infection.

The Royal Society for the Prevention of Cruelty to Animals (Causeway, Horsham, Sussex RH12 1HG) issues a series of pamphlets, costing 4p to 7p, giving advice and information about the care of different animals, including dogs and puppies, cats and kittens, hamsters, gerbils, guinea pigs, rabbits, tortoises and terrapins, parrots and tropical birds, aquaria; also *Care of your pets* which costs 40p.

quarantine kennels

Anti-rabies restrictions apply to the majority of mammals, such as dogs, cats, rabbits, hamsters, guinea pigs.

Provided you have suitable accommodation—a separate block of kennels and separate exercise runs, for instance—you could undertake to keep animals in quarantine for the period required by law: six months from the animal's arrival in this country.

Quarantine kennels must be under veterinary control and supervision: there are high standards to be met and setting up such kennels can be an expensive business.

Under the anti-rabies importation regulations, quarantine kennels have to be inspected and approved by the Ministry of Agriculture, Fisheries and Food. You have to have an arrangement with a veterinary surgeon (an MRCVS), approved by the Ministry, to come to inspect the animals every day.

Details of the requirements in England can be obtained from MAFF, Hook Rise South, Tolworth, Surbiton, Surrey KT6 7NF; in Scotland from DAFS, Chesser House, Gorgie Road, Edinburgh EH11 3AW; in Wales from WOAD, Plas Crug, Aberystwyth, Dyfed SY23 1NG.

The animal's owner has to arrange for it to be met at the appropriate airport or port by a special carrying agent, who will bring the animal to your premises in a specially enclosed container. When the six months is up, you issue a release certificate to the owner who can then take the animal home.

Having animals in quarantine means strict supervision to ensure that they have no contact with each other or other animals on your premises; this means separate eating and drinking utensils, and segregated quarters and exercise runs. The owners may want to come to visit their pet during the quarantine period, so you have to be prepared to arrange visiting times and to cope with the upset this may cause the animals—and the owners.

Although subject to Ministry control as far as your premises are concerned, you are free to charge what rates you choose, to cover the veterinary fees, extra care and responsibility that quarantine entails.

Rearing animals

For their produce as well as themselves, rearing chickens, ducks, turkeys, geese, rabbits, goats, are possibilities.

Check first of all whether there are any restrictive covenants affecting your property that could be invoked to stop you keeping animals at all, let alone for any commercial purposes.

Even with a large garden, a property in a built-up area may be restricted. On some council estates, animals that might produce problems regarding flies, smell, manure heaps, noise, are not allowed. You may need to get planning permission for change of use of your premises, and certainly if you intend to put up any huts, sheds or other outbuildings.

Make contact with a veterinary surgeon whose advice you can ask and on whose services you can then call whenever the need arises.

The general welfare of animals is covered by the Protection of Animals Acts 1911 to 1954. Under the Agriculture (Miscellaneous Provisions) Act 1968, it is an offence to cause unnecessary pain or distress to livestock on agricultural land. In this connection, livestock means any creature kept for the production of food, wool, skin or fur; agricultural land includes land on which animals are kept for the purposes of a trade or business.

The bi-monthly magazine *Practical Self-Sufficiency* (annual subscription £3.75, or 70p per copy, from Broad Leys Publishing Company, Widdington, Saffron Walden, Essex CB11 3SP) contains useful articles about choosing and keeping various types of animals, giving practical suggestions about their care, accommodation, feeding, safety. The magazine also carries advertisements from various suppliers of materials and equipment and foodstuffs, as well as hints from fellow 'farmers'.

Buy the feeding stuff you need in bulk, wherever possible. To transport it, you may need to hire or borrow a trailer or van; to store it, you will need plenty of space where it can be kept in good condition—be careful to protect it from rodents, which it may attract. Do not buy too much poultry food at one time: it becomes stale and loses vitamin content. About one month's supply at a time is sufficient.

Anyone keeping animals has to face up to the restriction their care imposes on holidays and time away from the premises. You need to be able to call on someone reliable to take over when you have to be away. An advertisement in a specialist magazine or the local paper might produce a suitable animal-sitter.

poultry

In legislative terms, poultry means turkeys, guinea fowls, ducks, geese and domestic fowls. The Ministry of Agriculture, Fisheries and Food (MAFF) and the Department of Agriculture and Fisheries for Scotland (DAFS) have codes of recommendations for the welfare of livestock, including no. 3 *Domestic Fowls*, no. 4 *Turkeys*. They are available free from MAFF, Hook Rise South, Tolworth, Surbiton, Surrey KT6 7NF and from DAFS, Chesser House, Gorgie Road, Edinburgh EH11 3AW.

You can ask your county MAFF poultry husbandry advisory officer for advice; get his address from the Ministry at Great Westminster House, Horseferry Road, London SW1P 2AE. (In Scotland, contact DAFS in Edinburgh.)

Shelter from the elements, and at night, must be provided. To keep marauders, particularly foxes, from getting at your flock, you will have to put up protective wiring. For free range poultry, you will need plenty of land and strong high fences.

The birds must have access to a constant supply of clean drinking water. Ducks and geese need a large area of grass (they will keep it nice and short for you); chickens, in addition to their feed, need grit—either artificially or by feeding in an area of rough ground.

Newcastle disease and fowl plague (or pest) are highly infectious diseases of poultry. They are notifiable diseases, and if you suspect either, you must inform the police or the local authority. A veterinary inspector will come to examine the birds. Vaccines can be used to control Newcastle disease, but fowl plague would necessitate compulsory slaughter (compensation is paid).

The Poultry Club (secretary at Virginia Cottage, 6 Cambridge Road, Walton-on-Thames, Surrey KT12 2DP) publishes a quarterly newsletter and a yearbook for its members, and can be asked for advice on the buying of pure breeds of poultry and waterfowl.

The British Poultry Federation (52–54 High Holborn, London WC1V 6SX) can put you in touch with the relevant association for producers of table and laying poultry—chickens, ducks, turkeys.

eggs and chickens
If you want the traditional pure breed hens, they will cost more to buy, and produce less, than the hybrid birds. Most types can be kept either in hen houses or on free range, but the light type of hybrid may be too 'flighty' for free range. You can charge more for eggs from free range birds (but they lay less in the winter).

The time to buy is when the birds are within a couple of weeks of laying, at about 18 weeks old. Day-old chicks are cheaper but are tricky to rear. They need to be housed in a warm and dry container with a controllable temperature and good lighting. Even so, there will probably be some losses during the first few days. To import hatching eggs or day-old (up to 72 hours) chicks into Scotland, quarantine regulations must be met, and fees paid, by the importer. DAFS can provide information about quarantine conditions and restrictions.

Eggs—like all food sold for human consumption—must meet the general legislative requirements for food quality, hygiene and description. To comply with EEC regulations for the marketing of hens' eggs, a producer has to become registered as a packing station or sell only to a registered packing station. However, a small-scale producer of eggs on his own farm can take advantage of the exemption for eggs passed directly to the consumer, or sold in a local public market or by door-to-door selling. The eggs should not be packed or graded into the quality and weight categories required by regulations for hens' eggs sold otherwise. This means that you can sell eggs from your own premises (put up a notice at the gate or nearby roadside) or through a local market. You will need a supply of trays or strong egg boxes (ask people to return them or bring their own).

Some ducks are bred for egg laying and produce a steady supply throughout the year. Ducks' eggs fetch more than hens' eggs. There is no legislation specific to the sale of ducks' eggs but any eggs for sale must be clean. It is therefore important to have plenty of clean straw on floors where ducks lay, otherwise the eggs get badly stained, and with the more porous shell there is a possible risk of salmonella.

If you are not too squeamish to kill your birds yourself, the Slaughter of Poultry Act lays down the methods of killing birds to be sold for human consumption. You may have to have extra accommodation and equipment to meet the requirements for slaughtering and preparing birds for sale.

Hygiene regulations apply to the selling of poultrymeat. You would be exempt from the requirements of these specific hygiene regulations if you sold your slaughtered birds to the final consumer direct or at markets in your neighbourhood or for direct consumption at restaurants, schools or other catering establishments or to retailers who sell direct. However, you must comply with the Food Hygiene (General) Regulations 1970. The basic principle behind these regulations is the avoidance of cross-contamination and the possibility of subsequent food poisoning. A code of practice (25p) for on-farm slaughter and marketing of poultry has been published jointly by the National Farmers' Union, the British Poultry Federation and the Environmental Health Officers' Association, and is available from the NFU, Agriculture House, Knightsbridge, London SW1X 7NJ.

goats

Goats can be kept for milk production by anyone with sufficient space to provide them with a weatherproof stable-type shed (one pen per goat), also grazing or a wired-in yard for exercise. Goats are adept at escaping and cannot be given the run of a garden or cultivated area: they would eat all green plants, trees and shrubs. They require much bulk food such as hay, and fresh green food—tree leaves and branches, surplus garden vegetables. A balanced corn ration is also required.

Goats demand regular daily attention if they are to flourish and milk well. Initially, it would be wise to start with a young adult female; a kid would need to be reared expertly to become a good milker.

You must learn the correct milking technique and about feeding and general care of the animals. Keeping goats is a seven-day-a-week occupation, and the routine must be adhered to. At holiday times, reliable arrangements must be made for their continued care and milking; otherwise, yields will drop and rarely improve later.

Foot-and-mouth disease is an acute infectious disease to which goats are susceptible. A suspected case must be reported immediately to the MAFF divisional veterinary officer, the local authority or the police. Affected animals must be slaughtered, and stringent precautionary restrictions are imposed on all premises for livestock in an area where an outbreak of foot-and-mouth disease occurs.

Details of membership and information on all aspects of goat-keeping can be obtained from the secretary of the British Goat Society, Rougham, Bury St Edmunds, Suffolk, or from the public relations officer, Blacknest Lodge, Sunninghill, Ascot, Berkshire. You can ask for the name and address of the secretary of a local goat society (send a stamped addressed envelope). There are articles on various aspects of keeping goats in back numbers of *Practical Self-Sufficiency*.

Goats' milk can be sold privately, or through a shop (in which case, your name and address must be on the carton or polythene bag containing the milk). You must meet normal hygiene requirements, but there are no statutory regulations governing the sale of goats' milk specifically, except that it must be labelled 'goat', and there is no price control. You may be in a position to make and sell yogurt or soft cheese to a local health food shop, dairy or market.

rabbits

There is currently a considerable demand for good quality table rabbits, primarily from the continent where the supply does not meet the demand.

You can literally start with two rabbits and build up to a herd of fifty or more (a doe can have six to eight litters a year). It is probably most appropriate to begin with a herd of about twenty does and two bucks. Buy does when they are about 12 weeks old; bucks a month older.

The initial setting-up costs include hutching with well-constructed wire floors, or wire cages in a garden shed or garage; feed hoppers; wooden nest boxes. You need a way of supplying fresh water, and should feed the animals on rabbit pellets supplemented with a bit of hay.

The Commercial Rabbit Association (Tyning House, Shurdington, Cheltenham, Glos GL51 5XF) has a comprehensive book on rabbit farming (£1, refunded on joining the Association) which includes the names of accredited breeders and market outlets.

Rabbits of acceptable weight and quality can be sold live to packers through regional collection points on a regular basis. Local butchers, too, are often willing to take live rabbits.

There are articles on rabbit farming for beginners in *Practical Self-Sufficiency*.

keeping bees

Keeping bees is a specialist activity which can be a source of income from the sale of honey and beeswax. Bees require regular but not daily attention, and feeding with sugar syrup at certain times, particularly if the weather is bad.

You need properly equipped hives, a sound bee veil, a smoker and a certain amount of honey extracting equipment and storage containers. The initial outlay is quite high, but do not be tempted to buy a secondhand hive unless you can be sure it is sound; it must be sterilised before being used.

The British Beekeepers Association offers advice for beginners or would-be beekeepers and will tell you about useful literature on the subject and give you the address of your nearest local beekeepers association. The BBKA publishes leaflets costing a few pence on, for example, swarm control, trees for bees, honey (obtainable from the secretary, 55 Chipstead Lane, Sevenoaks, Kent TN13 2AJ; send a stamped addressed envelope).

Most beekeepers associations publish magazines and newsletters, and there are many commercial publications about beekeeping.

There are also free Ministry of Agriculture, Fisheries and Food leaflets on bees and beekeeping such as advisory leaflet 283 *Advice to intending beekeepers* and 412 *Feeding bees.* MAFF bulletin no. 9 (75p) is an introduction to the theory and practice of the management of colonies of bees (MAFF publications are obtainable from Tolcarne Drive, Pinner, Middlesex HA5 2DT).

The International Bee Research Association (Hill House, Gerrards Cross, Bucks SL9 0NR) promotes the scientific study of bees; it publishes and distributes a wide range of publications.

Some local education authorities have an officer who can provide technical information on beekeeping and can be contacted through the local county college of agriculture. Practical beekeeping courses are run in some areas.

When honey is sold, it has to conform to standards for weight and presentation. There are composition and labelling regulations about honey (SI 1976 no. 1832; from HMSO, 22p), prescribing definitions and descriptions for honey sold in the UK. You will need screwtop jars or plastic containers (charge a returnable deposit on the jar or container).

The old combs can be rendered down and the beeswax sold for making candles, furniture polish and cosmetic creams.

For all your skill and knowledge, a long spell of bad weather can render beekeeping unprofitable. Therefore, do not rush into it, as it is too easy to spend more than you will get in return for honey or wax—or even mead.

Making mead is described in some detail in the Penguin book of *Home brewing and wine-making* by Tayleur (95p). The IBRA's pamphlet on mead by Brother Adam costs 40p.

'Made-wine' (that is, any liquor obtained from the alcoholic fermentation of a substance other than fresh grapes—which would include mead) cannot be sold unless you have an excise licence for your premises. Application for a licence should be made through the appropriate office of HM Customs and Excise (listed in the local telephone directory). Your premises and equipment will be inspected by a customs officer. The licence costs £5.25 for a year (which runs from 1 October) and excise duty is chargeable on the product at a fixed rate according to the alcoholic strength. Notice no. 162, *Wine and made-wine: production in the United Kingdom*, is available (free) from Customs and Excise offices.

Looking after children

Do not venture into the world of looking after children unless you are energetic, healthy, adaptable and ingenious, have a high noise tolerance, and are not too houseproud.

childminding

Most of the children needing to be looked after are under-fives whose parents are at work. Anyone receiving payment for looking after one or more children (not closely related to him or her), for more than two hours a day, has to register with the local authority social services department. This entails being visited at home, and providing the local authority with information about you and your premises and the care and facilities you are able to offer the children. You will be expected to have a safe, warm place for children to play, to have adequate kitchen and toilet facilities, to provide stimulating activities for them and take them out from time to time. Your health needs to be good; you will have to have a routine chest X-ray if you have not had one lately.

Before setting yourself up as a childminder on a regular basis, discuss the possibilities and what is involved with the local authority social worker. It would be worth joining the National Childminding Association (13 London Road, Bromley, Kent BR1 1DE; annual subscription £1 for individual membership). The Association's free leaflet *What is a childminder?* explains briefly the status and scope of a childminder, and the statutory and personal requirements. The NCMA has a form of contract you may like to use and arranges public liability insurance for registered childminders.

The BBC published a handbook for childminders to accompany a series of programmes in 1976: *Other people's children* (£1 from BBC Publications, 35 Marylebone High Street, London W1M 4AA).

You should have some basic knowledge of first aid and what to do in an emergency. The London borough of Hammersmith's environmental health education and home safety unit has produced a leaflet (20p) of hints for childminders on what action to take if certain symptoms or accidents occur, including what you should 'never' do.

You may need to buy some extra equipment and playthings: cots, perhaps small chairs or stools, potties, playpen, building bricks and other robust toys that can be shared by the children. You will have to organise your own household chores and demands around the hours when you have children to mind.

Once registered with the local authority, the social services department will put you on their vacancy list and you can advertise yourself direct. The local authority may stipulate that you cannot look after more than, say, four children under five together (including your own). The health visitor or a social worker may call to see you and your home and the children. Some social services departments give practical help such as toy kits and other equipment on loan, and some run training courses for childminders. A few local authorities employ child-minders direct.

You should keep a register of when each child comes to you, together with basic information about his date of birth, address, doctor's name and telephone number, parents' whereabouts.

Ensure that you always know where to contact either or both parents, when the child is going to be collected and by whom. Ask what the child can or cannot eat and any other essential factors, such as what the child calls the lavatory, when and for how long he sleeps during the day, what toy or other article is especially precious to him, warning signs of temper or tired-ness. A child who is ill should not be left with you. But you should alert your own general practitioner that you are child-minding, in case you need his or her help for a child who is taken ill or gets hurt while with you.

You are entitled to one-third of a pint of free milk a day for each child you are minding. Claim forms are available from the social services department.

It would be sensible to get to know other childminders in the district so that you can help each other out in times of illness or other emergencies or holidays.

There is no scale of charges laid down for childminding; in some areas, childminders have grouped together and agreed on a uniform rate. The National Childminding Association considers about £10 to £12 a week per child for whole-day care is reasonable (in 1979). You could charge more in certain circumstances—for providing extra meals, for example, or for keeping a child after 6pm, say, or overnight. You should stipulate payment in advance. Make clear at the outset whether you expect to receive holiday payment, either when the child is on holiday or when you are, and whether you will be paid if the child cannot come because of illness.

nursery groups

Someone who is a qualified nursery nurse or has similar experience in looking after children could set up a private day nursery group for pre-school children. You would have to register with the local authority social services department and meet the local authority's requirements about accommodation, catering arrangements and staffing (particularly the ratio of adults to children).

The British Association for Early Childhood Education (Montgomery Hall, Kennington Oval, London SE11 5SW) can be asked for advice and information on running a nursery school, and has various pamphlets and booklets that could be useful.

If you prefer to start up a playgroup, which is based on parent involvement and not intended to make a profit for anyone, contact the Pre-School Playgroups Association (Alford House, Aveline Street, London SE11 5DH) for advice and information. The PPA has published a pamphlet (40p) on starting a playgroup.

Taking lodgers

The size and layout of your house may enable you to take paying guests or lodgers. Before doing so, however, you ought to get in touch with the housing department of your local authority to check on their requirements for lodging establishments; some local authorities keep a register of what they call 'shared dwellings'. Ask whether planning permission is needed for the change of use or for any alterations you want to make to accommodate your lodgers. If your house is rented, you need the landlord's permission to take in lodgers, and also for any different fixtures you want to install, such as gas rings or extra washbasins.

If you have received an improvement or intermediate grant for work done to the house within the past, say, five years, you may be required to repay to the local authority part or all of it when you change the manner in which you are using your dwelling.

You have to advise your insurance company that you are taking in lodgers and you will automatically lose cover under your householder's policy for theft by someone who is on the premises legally, and for robbery without violent entry or exit from the premises. It is worth extending your insurance to cover your liability for injury or illness sustained by your lodgers and for damage that your negligence may cause to their property. You are not responsible for your lodgers' personal property, so you do not need to insure for its loss. But it would be fair to make it clear to your lodgers that if a thief who has broken in, or anyone else, steals their radio or any other item, it is their responsibility not yours to have insurance to cover the loss. With a larger establishment (say, of more than six bedrooms), you will need a special policy, designed for hotels and boarding houses.

When a householder does not have complete control over the occupants of the house, the fire risk increases significantly. Ask your fire prevention officer for advice on fire precautions to minimise the risk. Carrying out the fire prevention officer's recommendations may be expensive, but insurers may refuse to cover you unless you take the required fire precautions. You are legally obliged to obtain a fire certificate for premises where accommodation is provided for more than six people (staff and guests) and some of the sleeping accommodation is above the first floor or below the ground floor.

It would be wise to ask the local citizens advice bureau or a solicitor about the terms on which you let rooms in your house. The Rent Act affords a lot of protection to tenants, but holiday lettings are outside the legislation and so are arrangements where some services are provided—such as breakfast or other meals, laundry, cleaning. If you want to let rooms without providing meals, your tenants will have the protection of the Rent Act to some extent even when you are also living on the premises.

Get the Department of the Environment leaflets *Landlords and the law*, *Rooms to let* and *Shared houses*, which give relevant information about the legal aspects. DoE leaflets, which are free, are generally obtainable at citizens advice bureaux and housing advice centres, or you can write to the DoE, Building 3, Victoria Road, South Ruislip HA4 0NZ for copies. The corresponding leaflets for Scotland can be obtained from Scottish Development Department, Room 345, 2 St Andrew's Square, Edinburgh EH2 2BS.

To begin with, it would be sensible to take people on a short term basis: students, or visiting teachers or lecturers, research graduates, industrial personnel on training courses, apprentices, holiday makers, and such like. Get in touch with the personnel or accommodation officer of any nearby establishment where people are likely to come temporarily: university or technical college, manufacturing or computer firm, hospital, teacher or other training college, language school, repertory theatre. Someone from the organisation may want to come to interview you and inspect the accommodation you are offering. This contact means that you have some third party to refer to if there is any difficulty or disagreement between you and the lodger.

Alternatively, you can advertise direct, through the local paper or newsagents' boards, or just put up a sign at your own door (check on planning permission for this first). In a tourist area, the local authority may publish an accommodation list.

The regional tourist boards have a registration scheme for places providing accommodation in their regions. The schemes vary slightly, but each involves registration, providing full details of the accommodation offered and payment of a fee (except in Wales) which covers an entry in at least one tourist accommodation guide for the area, and the opportunity to be listed or advertise in other publications, countrywide or regional. You should contact the registration officer for your regional board; addresses are available from the national boards:

English Tourist Board
  4 Grosvenor Gardens, London SW1W 0DU
Scottish Tourist Board
  23 Ravelston Terrace, Edinburgh EH4 3EU
Wales Tourist Board
  Brunel House, 2 Fitzalan Road, Cardiff CF2 1UY
Northern Ireland Tourist Board
  River House, 48 High Street, Belfast BT1 2DS

In Northern Ireland, it is illegal to provide accommodation for the general public without being registered with the N.I. Tourist Board, whose staff will inspect the premises. Grants are available for the construction or improvement of establishments providing overnight accommodation. Details of the accommodation grants scheme can be obtained from the N.I. Tourist Board or the Department of Commerce (21 Linenhall Street, Belfast BT2 8BZ).

The English Tourist Board has published a development guide (no. 28) *Starting a small guest house or bed and breakfast business* (50p) covering legal and tax requirements, financial implications, sources of further information including other relevant development guides.

A similar guide published by the Scottish Tourist Board is *An introduction to bed and breakfast and guest house operation.*

The Wales Tourist Board publishes a series of advisory leaflets on, for example, receiving guests, taking foreign money, suppliers of catering equipment.

costs and commitments

If you are taking casual visitors, as you may be doing in a holiday area, you would probably find having a freezer worth the money, so that you do not get caught with insufficient supplies for a last-minute arrival. You will need good easily replaceable crockery, and a hot plate or heated trolley would make the exact timing for meals less critical. Towels, bedding and linen will be another major outlay; have non-iron or easy-care bed linen. An automatic washing machine would keep down laundry costs.

Someone should be in the house at all times, to receive unexpected calls or arrivals and to keep an eye on the place, its contents and inhabitants. You may have to let visitors have a key to come in late in the evening, but keep a close check on how many keys are being used and by whom. You may have to be prepared to lay down rules about bringing in friends.

Try to calculate the overhead expenses, including extra wear and tear on furnishings and linen, as accurately as you can, so that you include a reasonable proportion in your overnight or weekly charges. Be clear about extras, such as early morning tea, clothes washing, late meals or drinks. It would cost less in lighting and heating to share sitting and dining room with the lodgers, but you may prefer to keep your own household separate. A coin-box telephone may save a lot of arguing about telephone calls.

Depending on how committed you are willing to be, you can offer just breakfast, or an evening meal also or full board. Putting an electric kettle in the visitors' room enables them to make a cup of tea or coffee, provided you do not mind this in the bedroom.

Find out what other establishments in the neighbourhood are charging and adjust your own rates accordingly. You may decide to give an obviously superior service or deliberately ask less to attract custom. Decide whether to charge per room or per person and what to charge for a single person in a double room. It would be sensible to ask for a deposit or stipulate payment in advance from casual visitors.

The law requires that in an establishment with at least four bedrooms or eight beds to let, the maximum and minimum prices charged per night have to be displayed. (The requirements are set out in the Tourism (Sleeping Accommodation Price Display) Order 1977: SI 1877 from HMSO, 15p.)

foreigners

Lodgings for foreigners may be needed in your area, perhaps for groups (school children or adults) brought over by some specialist organisation to study in this country for a few weeks. You are paid by the organisers, not the students. The students go to english lessons during the day (you may have to arrange to get them to where they are being taught) and evening activities may be organised for them as well. You have to provide meals, or at least breakfast and dinner, and talk to the students (in english) to enable them to learn colloquial speech. But problems of communication and discipline can occur, and school children may be voracious or unruly, so make sure that you know where to reach the person in charge of the party at all times.

TAKING STOCK

Every so often you should pause in whatever you are doing and take stock to check what effect your freelance activities are having on

* your health and wellbeing, temper, attitude to others
* your ability to enjoy what you are doing
* your family or friends and their reactions
* your home and its state of care or neglect
* your bank balance

Allowing for inevitable family rows, debts, domestic crises and personal problems, if there is always more on the debit than the credit side, consider whether to stop.

DOING BADLY

Putting the whole operation into reverse includes informing your surviving customers, cancelling any standing advertisements, letting subscription and registration fees lapse, closing a business bank account if you had one. Cancel any special insurance policy or extension you had taken out because of your business activities. Tell the local authority where applicable, and get your rates put back to the domestic tariff.

Advertise any equipment that you want to get rid of, locally or in *Exchange and Mart*: check first what prices are being asked for similar secondhand goods.

Inform your inspector of taxes when you stop trading. And remember to allow for having to pay after the event for any tax due from your business takings. There are rules for setting off losses and for assessing tax for the closing years of a business, and the date you choose for the termination of your activities can make a difference to the tax for which you are liable. If you are finishing early in the tax year, it may be worth while not stopping until a few days after 5 April, to minimise any additional liabilities—always assuming that, when a venture is going so badly, it is feasible to carry on until a specific date.

What your tax bill is based on in closing years of business

your last-but-two tax year:	profit in your accounting year ending in the preceding tax year	*taxman's choice:* when you tell him that you have closed down your business, he can choose to base your tax bills for the last-but-two tax year and last-but-one tax year (but not just one of them) on the actual profit for each of these tax years. He will do this if it makes the total tax for the two years more.
your last-but-one tax year:	profit in your accounting year ending in the preceding tax year	
last tax year you are in business:	actual profit in that tax year	

(taken from the *Money Which? Tax-Saving Guide* March 1979)

If you are ceasing because you have run out of money and got into debt, you may decide on bankruptcy. This is a serious step to take. Before going ahead, go for advice to a citizens advice bureau who can give you detailed information about alternatives and procedure.

Bankruptcy

Any creditor who has obtained a judgment (a declaration by a court that money is due to him) against you can apply to the county court to issue and serve a bankruptcy notice on you. If you pay within 10 days of receiving such a notice, that is the end of the matter and you are not liable for any further costs. If not, the creditor can present a bankruptcy petition (minimum debt £200) at any time within the following three months. This will cost him about £250. If you pay up at this stage, you will have to pay about £135 of the creditor's costs.

A debtor can present a petition for his own bankruptcy at any time; the court fee is £5 plus a deposit of £50 (in cash). You are declared bankrupt immediately the requisite forms have been completed at the court, and no further action can be taken by creditors to press for their money. Although bankruptcy releases you from all past debts, the process is very harrowing, and should be avoided if at all possible.

If bankruptcy is proceeded with, a receiving order will be made, appointing the official receiver (an officer of the court) as receiver of your assets. You are required to provide (with the help of an accountant or the official receiver) a sworn statement of your assets and liabilities, including details of all your creditors. An advertisement is put in the *London Gazette* and your local newspaper.

Under the Bankruptcy Acts, it is a criminal offence not to have kept proper books of accounts during the two years prior to the presentation of a bankruptcy petition or, having kept the books, not to have preserved them. The definition of proper books is that they must exhibit or explain the transactions and financial position of the business, including a book recording all cash received and paid, and, where the business deals in goods, there must be statements of annual stock takings and accounts of all goods sold and purchased showing the names of the buyers and sellers (except for retail sales).

At a creditors' meeting, which will be called to decide whether to press on with the bankruptcy claim, you can put forward a scheme of arrangement for clearing the debts. A trustee and committee for the creditors may be appointed to supervise you.

If there is a public examination in court (the county court or, in London, the High Court), you will be questioned by the official receiver and may be cross-examined by creditors and trustee.

Whether or not there is a public examination, the official receiver will apply for an adjudication order. This transfers all property and assets to the creditors' trustee (or to the official receiver if a trustee has not been appointed). All your assets, furniture and possessions can then be realised on behalf of your creditors. However, items necessary for your obligations to dependants, tools of your trade, up to £250-worth of clothes and bedding, cannot be claimed. Jointly owned property, such as the family home, may have to be sold to realise the debts, and the other spouse cannot normally prevent the sale although he or she will be able to claim an appropriate share of the money gained.

A bankrupt has to disclose that he is an undischarged bankrupt if he wishes to obtain credit from anyone for more than £50, and cannot carry on any trade or business without disclosing his circumstances, even under a different name. Nor can he run a bank account without the consent of the Department of Trade.

A bankrupt can apply to the court at any time for discharge from bankruptcy. The official receiver notifies the creditors of the application, which is also advertised in the *London Gazette*. He also files a report on the bankrupt's conduct. There will be another hearing and examination in open court before a decision is made to grant, suspend or refuse an order for discharge. The order may provide for payment of all or part of the outstanding debts. Under the Insolvency Act 1976, the official receiver has to initiate a review after five years of bankruptcy if the bankrupt has not applied for his own discharge.

Bankruptcy is a lengthy and fairly expensive procedure, so for a relatively small debt, creditors may be willing to come to some alternative arrangement.

DOING WELL

One of the snags of success is that you may find yourself with more orders than you can fulfil,at least to the same standard as your original. You are then faced with the tricky decision whether to cause resentment and loss of custom by refusing work or to risk the complications of taking on a colleague to share the work (and the proceeds) or employ someone either in your home or as an outworker.

Employing others

The role of employer carries certain statutory responsibilities regarding tax, third party and employer's liability, conditions of work, contract of employment, national insurance.

For class 1 national insurance contributions, which employer and employed are statutorily obliged to pay, you have to pay 13.5 per cent of the employee's wages between £19.50 and £135 a week (1979/80) as the employer's share of contributions. Leaflet NP 15, obtainable from social security offices, is an employer's guide to national insurance contributions and leaflet NI 208 gives current rates of contributions.

An employer has to pay both his and his employee's contributions but is entitled to deduct the employee's share from the wages he pays. An official deduction card (P 11) has to be completed each time an employee gets paid. Instructions on the use of this official deduction card are given on another card (P 8) issued by the tax office to employers.

Employees over pension age (60 for a woman, 65 for a man) are no longer liable to make national insurance contributions but you would not be saved your share if you employ someone older. And you would still have to cope with their tax under the PAYE system. Leaflet P 7, *Employer's Guide to PAYE*, is available from the local tax inspector's office.

In addition to tax and national insurance responsibilities, an employer is obliged by law to take out and maintain an approved insurance policy to cover liability for bodily injury or disease that an employee may suffer in the course of the employment. A short guide to the Employer's Liability (Compulsory Insurance) Act is available from the Health and Safety Executive, 1 Chepstow Place, London W2 4TF.

Enlisting members of your own family simplifies the employment situation. You can arrange to recompense them in kind or at a level below the thresholds for tax and national insurance. However, the authorities may be suspicious of payments that are only a few pence below the minima—for instance, paying your daughter £19.25 a week which would avoid national insurance contributions. Where a husband employs his wife, wife's earned income allowance can be claimed to set against her earnings for tax. The taxman will want some evidence that the wife actually does the work she is paid for and that she has received the money for it. But where it is the wife who runs the business and her husband works for her, no extra tax allowance can be claimed.

To begin with, it may be better not to commit yourself to providing work for anyone for a set period or permanently.

Anyone who works part-time for less than 16 hours a week is outside the employment protection legislation. If you employ someone to work for more hours a week, you must, to comply with the Employment Protection (Consolidation) Act 1978, give a written contract of employment after 13 weeks; the employee is eligible to claim compensation if you have to make him or her redundant or a dismissal is proved to have been unfair.

It is simpler to use people on a freelance basis, who retain their self-employed status, in which case tax and national insurance are their concern. You are merely, as it were, an intermediary between the outworker and your client.

The boot is on the other foot if you become a supplier for an outworker—who does typing, soft toymaking, assembly, finishing or whatever—and you should do as you would be done by.

FORMING A COMPANY

If you are thinking of forming a company, it is worth getting in touch with one of the regional centres of the Department of Industry's small firms information service. A similar service is provided in Northern Ireland by the Department of Commerce.

The Welsh Development Agency has a small business unit with offices throughout Wales offering general advice to expanding small concerns, and a specialist technical service (for which a charge is made); the unit can make loans in suitable cases. Address: Welsh Development Agency, Small Business Unit, Treforest Industrial Estate, Pontypridd, mid-Glamorgan CF37 5UT (tel: Treforest 2666).

In Scotland, the Scottish Development Agency provides specialist help for small manufacturing, craftwork and certain service enterprises. It gives marketing and promotion advice and management and technical assistance, and operates a small loan scheme. Address: Scottish Development Agency, Small Business Division, 102 Telford Road, Edinburgh EH4 2NP (tel: 031-343 1911).

The small firms information service regional centres are at:

57 Bothwell Street, Glasgow G2 6TU
tel: 041-248 6014 (freefone 846)

16 St. David's House, Wood Street, Cardiff CF1 1ER
tel: Cardiff 396116 (freefone 1208)

Newgate Shopping Centre, Newcastle upon Tyne NE1 5RH
tel: Newcastle 25353 (freefone 529)

Peter House, Oxford Street, Manchester M1 5AN
tel: 061-832 5282 (freefone 6005)

5 Royal Exchange House, City Square, Leeds LS1 5PQ
tel: Leeds 445151 (freefone 5361)

48–50 Maid Marian Way, Nottingham NG1 6GF
tel: Nottingham 49791 (freefone 4062)

53 Stephenson Street, Birmingham B2 4DH
tel: 021-643 3344 (freefone 4054)

35 Wellington Street, Luton LU1 2SB
tel: Luton 29215 (freefone 372)

Colston Centre, Colston Avenue, Bristol BS1 4UB
tel: Bristol 294546 (freefone 9910)

65 Buckingham Palace Road, London SW1W 0QX
tel: 01-828 2384 (freefone 2079)

They provide booklets on various aspects of running a small business, and you can telephone for advice or information on any specific query about setting up a business. The freefone number is obtainable in the region only via the operator.

One of their free booklets *Starting in business* includes an explanation of:

* being a sole trader: 'you are totally responsible for your business; you take all the profits (after tax) but must bear all the losses. Creditors suing you to recover debts incurred as a result of your business activity can also claim against your personal property.'

* a partnership: 'partnerships are liable for the debts of the business up to the sum of the total personal assets of each partner. Any agreement entered into by any one partner in the course of business is fully binding upon all the others, even if they have counselled him against such action.'

  It is better to get the advice of a solicitor or accountant who is knowledgeable in the subject before forming a partnership.

* a limited company: 'a limited company is a legal entity in its own right; it can both sue and be sued. . . . The owners of the company—the shareholders—are not liable for the company's debts to the extent of their means, but only to the extent of the face value of the shares in the company issued to them.'

  This is generally a good option because of liability being limited and because it may be easier to get bank loans once you are incorporated. In practice, the directors may have to give guarantees to the bank, thus making their personal assets liable for part of the company's debts.

If you decide to try forming a new limited company in the business name you have been using so far, or by registering a new one, you will probably need help from a company registration agent or a solicitor or an accountant. Ten pages of *Notes for the guidance of registered companies* (from 'accounts' to 'winding up') are available from the Companies Registration Office, Companies House, Crown Way, Maindy, Cardiff CF4 3UZ. The Scottish Registrar of Companies is at 102 George Street, Edinburgh EH2 3DJ.

The quickest, and probably the cheapest, way is to buy a ready-made limited company off the shelf, as it were, through a company registration agent (they are listed in the telephone directory yellow pages).

Registration agents register incorporated companies with fictitious names at Companies House, members of the agent's staff being registered as the director and secretary. Someone who wants to buy a company can choose from the list of names, then complete forms (4A and 9B) recording the new director and secretary and address for the registered company. You pay the fees, and the agent does the rest. The name of the company, the memorandum and articles of association, can all be altered at any time to suit the function of the real company, provided the registrar of companies allows.

Some organisations you could contact, in case membership would be useful, include:

National Federation of Self Employed and Small Businesses

branches throughout the UK, head office
32 St Annes Road West, Lytham St Annes, Lancs FY8 1NY
tel: 0253-720911; London office 01-439 8546

The Association of Independent Businesses

(formerly the Smaller Businesses Association)
Europe House, World Trade Centre, London E1 9AA
tel: 01-481 8669

The Alliance of Small Firms and Self-employed People

(formerly the Association of Self-employed People)
279 Church Road, London SE19 2QQ
tel: 01-653 4798

The Institute of Small Business

Tower Suite, 1 Whitehall Place, London SW1A 2HD
tel: 01-930 5577

APPLYING FOR A PATENT

If, deliberately or by chance, you find that you have invented some gadget or machine or method which is totally new and is capable of industrial or agricultural application, you may want to patent it, to prevent exploitation of the same idea by others.

The procedure for obtaining a patent is fairly complicated, from filing the application (which protects your invention for one year) to publication and grant of the patent. Fees have to be paid at various stages: for example, £5 on making the application, £40 for a preliminary examination and search. An official pamphlet *Applying for a patent*, giving detailed information on the procedure and conditions, is available free from the Comptroller, The Patent Office, 25 Southampton Buildings, London WC2A 1AY, who can also supply application forms and a list of current fees.

There are patent agents who will deal with the whole procedure (for a fee). A list of registered patent agents can be looked at in the Patent Office or you can buy it for 50p from the Chartered Institute of Patent Agents, Staple Inn Buildings, London WC1V 7PZ.

A patent lasts for 20 years, provided you pay an annual renewal fee. Even if you are unable to use your invention to produce a gadget, machine or process yourself, you can exploit it by granting somebody else a licence to use it, or by selling the patent outright.

VALUE ADDED TAX

Once the taxable turnover (the total you charge customers, not the net profit you may make) of your total business activities has exceeded certain limits, you are required to notify HM Customs and Excise, and will be registered for value added tax.

registration limits
If at any time there are reasonable grounds for believing that your taxable turnover will exceed £10000 in the next 12 months, you must immediately notify Customs and Excise.

At the beginning of each calendar quarter (1 January, 1 April, 1 July, 1 October), you should consider your taxable turnover in the immediately preceding quarter:

did the taxable turnover exceed
 £ 3500 in the last quarter?
 £ 6000 in the last two quarters?
 £ 8500 in the last three quarters?
 £10000 in the last four quarters?

If the answer to any of these questions is 'yes', you must notify within ten days of the end of the quarter. Unless you can satisfy Customs and Excise that you will not have a turnover of more than £10000 in the full year (that is, the past quarter(s) and the remainder of the year), you will be liable for VAT from the obligatory registration date. This is 21 days from the quarterly review date on which any of the limits was exceeded—even if you had not realised and had not been charging your customers VAT on their bills.

Look up the nearest main VAT office of HM Customs and Excise in your local telephone directory and ask for advice on the procedure and timing for registration. The VAT office can let you have current copies of their notices no. 700 (general guide) and no. 701 (scope and coverage) and any others that may be relevant to your situation (for example, on secondhand transactions or on supplies through agents); also the form (VAT 1) of notification of liability to be registered for value added tax.

Once you are registered, you must pay to HM Customs and Excise a percentage of the price you charge customers or clients for supplying goods or services which are classified as taxable at a positive rate for VAT purposes. At present, some groups of goods and services are exempt from VAT; of the positive rated ones, some are zero-rated, the rest are rated at the standard rate (now 15 per cent).

You have to charge value added tax not only on all taxable goods you supply but on any taxable service for which you charge: for example, hairdressing, providing accommodation or catering, doing repairs, giving professional advice, buying or selling as an agent. You can charge your customers for the appropriate VAT, either by including it in the total price or by showing it separately.

Even if some or all of the goods you deal in are zero-rated, you have to notify Customs and Excise when your turnover reaches the VAT threshold.

keeping records
You have to put your VAT registration number on all invoices and are required to keep special VAT records. Either incorporate a VAT column in your cashbooks, or buy VAT approved record books, so that you can transfer the information to the form of return of value added tax which the VAT office will send you to use each quarter. This return has to be sent to the VAT

Central Unit, Alexander House, 21 Victoria Avenue, South-end-on-Sea, Essex SS99 1AA, not to the local office. Take a photocopy, or ask for a supply of spare VAT return forms so that you can complete a duplicate each time. This will enable you to refer to your declaration should there be a query when the VAT man calls to check on you.

You are required by law to produce records and associated papers referring to your business at any time when requested to do so by a Customs and Excise officer. VAT surveillance is strict, and it is important to understand fully what is expected of you and what and how to charge. The VAT man can descend on you unannounced at any time to check all your accounts. There are severe penalties for failure to comply and they are ruthlessly administered.

While you are not a registered trader for VAT, you can include as part of a claim for a tax allowance on business expenses or capital items any value added tax you have had to pay. But once you are VAT-registered, do not include the VAT on any such items—you claim it back through the VAT system.

voluntary registration
Even when your taxable turnover is below the limit for obligatory registration, it could be worthwhile to be registered voluntarily because this may enable you to reclaim any VAT you have been charged on any purchase or expense in the course of your business—for example, the tax on petrol (your claim for this should tie up with your claim for tax allowance on your use of the car for business).

Before such registration is allowed, you will have to satisfy Customs and Excise that you have a genuine and continuing need for registration, and you will have to accept in advance certain conditions imposed on the registration. Once registered, however small your turnover, you will have to keep proper records for VAT, account for VAT you have charged and render regular VAT returns.

de-registration
After being registered for two years, you can ask your VAT office to cancel your registration if your taxable supplies—that is, total value of all goods and/or services you supply—have been £8500 or less in each of the last two years, or £2500 or less in each of the last eight quarters. You may also request cancellation if your taxable supplies are not expected to exceed £8500 in the coming year. The local VAT office can let you have an explanatory leaflet about *Cancelling your registration*.

INDEX

CONSUMER PUBLICATIONS

Cutting your cost of living
helps you take care of the pence—and the pounds, too. It advises you on how to cut down your spending by adapting your shopping habits, how to make small savings (on food, heating, gardening) and larger ones (on travel, do-it-yourself, holidays, luxuries), giving warnings about false economies and guidance on how to take advantage of what is available free.

Dismissal, redundancy and job hunting
covers the legal aspects of redundancy and unfair dismissal, explains compensation and what happens if a claim is taken to an industrial tribunal. The book also gives advice on the practical and personal aspects of being unemployed, on claiming unemployment benefit and on the various stages of job hunting.

Living through middle age
gives advice on how to take care of yourself between the ages of 40 and 60 when the body is going through many physical changes. It tells you how to minimise any adverse effects such as problems with hair, skin and teeth, and also advises on health risks, such as being overweight. There is a section on the menopause, and on psychological problems for both men and women.

The legal side of buying a house
covers the procedure for buying an owner-occupied house with a registered title in England or Wales (not Scotland) and describes the part played by the solicitors and building society, the estate agent, surveyor, Land Registry, insurance company and local authority. It takes the reader step by step through a typical house purchase so that, in many cases, he can do his own conveyancing without a solicitor; it also deals with the legal side of selling.

Extending your house

describes what is involved in having an extension built on to a house or bungalow, explaining what has to be done, when and by whom. It explains how the Building Regulations affect the position and design of an extension, and how to apply to the local authority for planning permission and Building Regulations approval.

Central heating

helps you to choose central heating for your home, tells you how to find a good installer to carry out the work and gives details of the equipment involved. The book discusses the merits of the different fuels and helps you assess their relative running costs. It highlights the importance of improving insulation, to keep the heat in. There is a section dealing with problems and hazards that might arise after your central heating is installed.

Claiming on home, car and holiday insurance

gives you the information you need to know when filling in a claim form and interprets some of the terms and phrases you may be faced with when claiming, such as averaging, betterment and subrogation. The book specifies what the various policies do and do not cover.

Avoiding back trouble

tells you about the spine and what can go wrong with it, concentrating mainly on the lower back; gives hints on general care of the back when sitting, standing, lifting, carrying, doing housework, gardening, driving, and deals with an attack of back trouble, specialist examination and treatment.

On getting divorced
explains the procedure for getting a divorce in England or
Wales, and how, in a straightforward undefended case, it can
be done by the postal procedure and without paying for a
solicitor. The legal advice scheme and other state help for
someone with a low income is described, and there is advice
on coping with the home and children in reduced circumstances.
Calculations for maintenance and division of property are given
with details of the orders the court may make for financial
settlements between the divorcing couple and for arrangements
about the children.

An ABC of motoring law
is a guide through the maze of criminal legislation which affects
the motorist—in Scotland as well as England and Wales. It
describes the offences you could commit, the people and procedures involved, and the penalties you could face. The book
is arranged alphabetically, from alcohol to zigzag lines. Clear
charts guide you through procedures such as reporting an
accident or appearing in court.

Which? way to slim
is the complete guide to losing weight and staying slim. The
book separates fact from fallacy, and gives a balanced view of
essentials such as suitable weight ranges, target weights, exercise, and the advantages and disadvantages of the different
methods of dieting. The book highlights the dangers of being
overweight and gives encouraging advice about staying slim.

Where to live after retirement
gives general advice about planning realistically for your future
housing needs and assessing the suitability of your present
home—whether it can be adapted, and the financial aspects
involved. It gives detailed information on the various types of

accommodation available should you decide to move, including residential homes.

What to do when someone dies
explains factually and in detail all that may need to be done: getting a doctor's certificate, reporting a death to the coroner, registering a death and getting the various death certificates. Burial and cremation are discussed, and funeral arrangements, and the national insurance benefits that can be claimed.

Wills and probate
stresses the advisability of making a will, explains how to prepare one, sign it and have it witnessed. It gives examples of different types of wills showing consideration for the effects of capital transfer tax. The section about probate deals in detail with the administration of an estate without a solicitor, and illustrates the various situations and problems that might arise.

other Consumer Publications include:
Pregnancy month by month
The newborn baby
Health for old age
Having an operation
Treatment and care in mental illness
How to sue in the county court

Consumer Publications are available from
Consumers' Association, Caxton Hill, Hertford SG13 7LZ
and from booksellers.